PROCESSED FOR HIS PURPOSE - PURPOSED FOR HIS PROMISE

LARRY EDWARD BIRCHETT, JR.

PROCESSED FOR HIS PURPOSE
PURPOSED FOR HIS PROMISE

Larry Edward Birchett, Jr.

ISBN: 978-0615931531 (Treasures of the Heart Publishing)
Copyright @ January 2014

Contact and booking information:
harvesthouserestorationcenter@gmail.com
www.harvesthouserestorationcenter.com

All rights reserved.

All scripture is from The New King James Version or King James Version unless otherwise indicated.

Cover Design and Photography by: CTS Graphic Design/
www.ctsgraphics.net

Printed in the United States of America. The contents of this book may not be reproduced whether in whole or part, stored in a retrieval system, or transmitted in any form without the prior written consent of the publisher.

Table of Contents

Foreword……………………………………………...5

Acknowledgements…………………………………..7

The Man in the Maze………………………………...9

Processed for Purpose………………………………17

The Cloud and the Fire…………………………...23

Hidden Wisdom……………………………………..35

The Saint…………………………………………...51

Godly Leadership……………………………………65

The Law of the Spirit of Life/The Law of Sin & Death……...71

Spiritual Authority & Leadership……………………..77

Mirage…………………………………………… 91

Perspective………………………………………..99

Weeds in your Garden……………………………… 107

Indecent Proposal……………………………………119

Matimba and Kanya's Pride…………………………135

Tips and Spiritual Keys……………………………..142

DEDICATION

This book is dedicated to the person who is ready to give up because they've lost hope in every thing that is good, pure, and even holy in life and feel as if they will never reach their purpose. I'm here to let you know that God loves you so much that He stepped out of eternity into time and directed me to write this book just for you. He's drawn you to this book on purpose because there are no accidents in God, He does everything on PURPOSE. He has something to tell you. Enjoy your reading. I dedicate this book to you.

Foreword

To God be All Glory and honor for all the great things He has done, It is with great honor that I write the foreword for this powerful book "Processed for His Purpose - Purposed for His Promise." This man of God is my wonderful spouse, Pastor and friend. When I first met Larry Birchett, Jr. I knew that there was something different about him. He is a man of discipline, obedience, faithfulness, integrity and most of all a mighty man of God. As his wife and friend, I am so thrilled to see all that God is doing in his life. Larry has first hand experience of being processed for His purpose.

Throughout our times being together, I have seen Larry at his mountain high and valley lows but one thing for sure is that he has shown himself strong in God. The title of this book says it all, and I can assure you that your perception of your process will begin to change after reading this powerful and dynamic book.

Larry Birchett, Jr. has written a book that is very timely in that it teaches us how to understand that we are being processed for HIS purpose. Many times we tend to give up because we lack the understanding in a spiritual sense, but I can truly say that Larry Birchett, Jr. is one of the most qualified persons I know to endeavor to write a book about, Processed for His Purpose - Purposed for His Promise. The fact that he is my husband makes him qualified, and yes, I am biased, but I have watched him for the past six years of his life as God has been taking him through the Process into his Purpose. I believe that you can only truly edify people through your own experiences and that is what makes this book so unique.

Processed for His Purpose - Purposed for His Promise, keeps you yearning for more as one of the most common questions that individuals ask themselves is, "What is Purpose?' Well Larry broke that thing down and it made me realize that *"Purpose is the mission God predestined for you to accomplish, while you are here on earth. He planned it before the foundations of the earth and for this reason he created you. You cannot create it or find it by yourself; it is revealed to you by God."* So as you read each chapter of this powerful book understand that you too are being processed for His Purpose. And we know that all things work together for good to those who love God, to those who are the called according to His purpose. Romans 8:28 (NKJV)

Beloved, understand that this book will bring forth a changed mindset, it will allow you to look into the Spiritual realm and as Pastor Larry Birchett, Jr. states *"you will begin to approach life as a victor and not a victim."* Just know that every page of this book has been intricately placed into the man of God by the Wisdom of the Holy ghost to edify and equip you for your purpose. You might have to go through a little pain while you're going through your *process* but through the pain you will birth forth Gods promise.

Joanna Birchett
Co-Pastor – Harvest House Restoration Center, Carlisle, PA
CEO – Gospel 4 U Network, Carlisle, PA
Author of *Defeat Was Never an Option*

Acknowledgments

I'd like to thank the Holy Spirit for pulling out the grace that God has attributed and imbedded in me while I was in my mother's womb for the purpose of this book I have been inspired to aspire for my highest self in God as He continues to reveal to me and in me His purpose for my life.

I'd like to thank my gorgeous and gifted wife, Joanna, for her love and support of me via this book and everything else that God has placed in my heart. You're always there my love and it means the world to me. It's you and me to the end of time *babygirl.*

I'd like to thank my children who inspire me with their very existence and unconditional love towards me. I love you all so much and I pray that as your father that I've been the champion that every father is supposed to be for their sons and daughters.

I'd like to thank my parents Dr. Rev. Arlene Paulette Birchett and Reverend Larry Birchett, Sr. for pure love and dealing with me in love even when I didn't deserve it. I love you two so much and I pray that my effect on my children will be nearly as much as your Godly examples have been to me. I honor you for rearing me and my beautiful little sister Nija Birchett in the way that we should go.

I'd like to thank my spiritual father and mother Apostle Earl Palmer and Pastor Maria Palmer for helping me develop a lot of the skills that I will be referring to in this book and for always being a source of encouragement and strength.

Lastly, I'd like to thank the greatest church in Pennsylvania, Harvest House Restoration Center for encouraging, inspiring, and obliging me to explore what God has for me. It is an honor to be the under shepherd of such an awesome congregation. You all are such a blessing to me.

CHAPTER 1

The Man in the Maze

Just because you're alive doesn't mean you're living.
Larry Birchett, Jr.

There was once a Jewish parable about a man named Jacob. Jacob rubbed his eyes. Every path he took was a dead end. He was hungry and tired, and now it looked as if he would remain in this maze forever! "If the king wants to amuse himself by setting up such a complex maze of paths, of which only one path reaches the palace, why must I suffer?" thought Jacob to himself as he again reached a dead end and had to about-face.

Suddenly he heard his name being called from high above. "Jacob, Jacob! Look up here!" The sun blinded him as he tried to squint up at the source of the voice. At last, he caught sight of a bearded old sage perched on the roof of the palace, frantically pointing out the path to take.

"Why should I listen to him?" Jacob thought to himself. "Who does he think he is, telling me what to do? It's a free country and I can blunder into as many dead ends as I please! *And suffer the consequences, too!"*

Jacob then heard the words of the sage. "I have gone through the king's maze and found the one path leading to the palace. From my vantage point on the roof, I can view all of the paths in front of you. If you follow my advice, you will be in the palace very shortly and receive a juicy reward. If you reject my advice, you might remain in the maze for the rest of your life!"

This analogy of course is referring to how many of us try to maneuver through the maze of life in our own strength, with our own ideas and methods, even though billions of people have lived before us and have demonstrated which routes are traditionally risky, dangerous, and downright wrong. There are some individuals that still think that they would fare better if they go about things in their own way. Proverbs 19:21(NIV) says it like this: *Many are the plans in a man's heart, but it is the LORD's purpose that prevails.*

God has a purpose for every avenue and every corridor that we go down in life. Every divine connection and/or disconnection is directed and allowed by Him. So we have to pay attention to the plan and purpose of God for **our** lives and walk accordingly. Just because you have been through some pretty rough things doesn't mean that someone has been trying to make you fail. It doesn't mean that you're destined to fail. It could actually just be part of **your** process. It could mean that you're *"in process"*; a term that I use to explain when God has placed you right in the middle of the thing or situation that He will use to develop you. Something intentional that God had always planned for you to have to go through or overcome. **Some struggles**

are sent for a purpose and on purpose to process you. Your purpose will make the process bearable because it's the process that actually leads you to your purpose. Once your purpose is identified you can progress onto your *place* of promise. Without process you can't progress and without progression you will never reach your potential and can never truly evolve.

God most of the times utilizes our failures to fertilize our future. Sometimes life in general, circumstances, events, and even people will throw stones in your path. It depends on **you** how you will respond however, after these attacks. The same stones and bricks that have been thrown at you can either be looked at as an insurmountable wall of difficulties or a divine bridge to success.

Stop looking at life with the lens of the defeated and remember that God has already spoken Romans 8:37 concerning you specifically that *you are more than a conqueror*! He has spoken to you specifically *that NO weapon that is formed against you shall prosper and EVERY tongue that rises up against you in judgment, you shall condemn.* Isaiah 54:17

Approach life as a victor not a victim; understanding that we have the keys to life and death in our tongue. **Understand that God wants us to succeed.** *Beloved, I wish above all things that thou mayest prosper and be in health, even as thy soul prospereth. 3 John 1:2(KJV)*

Many of us are like the man in the maze, looking for the purpose of our life in all of the wrong places. The sage is an example of true divine Godly wisdom that God has placed and made accessible at critical points of our lives. Some heed to God's wisdom and probably more than those who heed, are they like the man in the parable, who decide that they can make more out of life than anyone else who ever lived by doing it their own way; and yet very few people who feel this way succeed.

So when the wisdom appears; and this wisdom can come in the form of advice from a friend, a teacher, a wise old man/woman, Rabbi, Pastor, or other clergyman, and even a poet/philosopher/lyricist; we have to be able to discern the wisdom from the foolishness, the distraction from divine direction and we shouldn't be so fast to dismiss every word of instruction that comes our way. Don't dismiss everything that is contrary to your way of thinking. That old "sage" can actually be God trying to impart understanding and direction in your life. In some instances God may actually be trying to save and/or extend your life.

The blockade on the road or dead end could be God's divine way of saying, *go back the other way my child, there's nothing good for you on this route.* **I'm a firm believer in the fact that sometimes you have to backup to go forward.** Some of us will try to knock down the wall and realize that it's unmovable in our own strength. God loves when we get to this point because that's when we have to put all of our trust in Him.

Only God can demolish some obstacles that He **allows** to be placed in our path. Even when He orders the destruction of the barrier because of His grace and wanting us to find our true path we then have to walk over the debris and carry the dirt, the dust, and the pain that was experienced because of the effort it took to get through the demolished areas of our purpose, the demolished areas of our lives. And this isn't easy; it takes a lot of effort to maneuver through these demolished areas.

Sometimes beloved, you will have to retrace your steps and find out where you started going awry and then take an alternate route. It takes resolve to go through these kind of seasons. We have to purpose in our hearts that even though this is going to be painful, I'm moving forward. All success is intentional. Nobody becomes a success without effort. True success is always intentional never an accident.

Pay the Cost

In everything there is a process and the process that it will take for God to order the removal of a thing is sometimes a costly one. The response that you are waiting for from heaven will cost you something beloved. I'm smiling as I'm writing this because this is one of the most unpopular messages that I sometimes have to tell people. Why? Because we live in a generation where we think somebody owe us something. And let me get the record straight, I'm not talking about money! I'm talking about spiritual currency such as praise, worship and integrity of spirit even when no one is watching. God loves authenticity. I always remind and sometime instruct the saints of God in church services where the spirit is high that *if they want something from heaven, something has to first leave this earth!* In order to get God involved in our battles we have to provide the atmosphere that He likes. He has told us in His Word that He inhabits the praises of His people. Consider the following verse; *"But thou art holy, O thou that inhabitest the praises of Israel." Psalm 22:3(KJV)* Therefore if we are smart, every time that we need a sure intervention from God in our lives we would praise Him even harder and exalt His name even higher than we normally do.

What am I saying? Beloved, I'm saying that if you're at a dead end start praising your way out! God is waiting to hear the sound of an authentic praise that can only come from your spirit. This type of praise summons the very fabric of heaven into your atmosphere and every demon in hell has to wilt and flee at His presence. Every barrier will have to crumble.

If we miss the spiritual barriers and signs we might be adding to the amount of time it was suppose to take us to get where we're going. Don't violate God's stop signs. Ask God for discernment and while you're seeking God for direction don't forget to give Him his praise. **The passion of your praise while you're "in process" will determine the level of empowerment that you will receive after it's over.** What am I saying? I'm saying that we're supposed to grow from level to level and then we should allow ourselves to be catapulted from that level into another dimension.

God wants us to enter new dimensions in Him and He accomplishes this by the trials and experiences that we go through. The scriptures put it this way; *And not only that, but we also glory in tribulations, knowing that tribulations produces perseverance, and perseverance, character, and character, hope. Now hope does not disappoint, because the love of God has been poured out in our hearts by the Holy Spirit who was given to us. ~ Romans 5:3*

When we are *in process*, we are supposed to work our faith like a football player works the weight bench. Resistance creates growth. The more weights you lift the bigger your muscles become and the stronger you get. The longer you run on a consistent basis the more endurance your body gets and the better your cardiovascular condition becomes. The spiritual process that we normally go through is exactly the same. When we're in tough situations our faith is supposed to be strengthened and increased because we're utilizing it. If we're whining through the process we will likely just be moved from one "weight bench" to another.

Consider this verse; *For our light and momentary troubles are achieving for us an eternal glory that far outweighs them all. 2 Corinthians 4:17, (NIV).* Aren't you glad that your troubles and trials are only temporary? In fact, God is telling us that they are momentary. Compared with eternity, our troubles don't last long at all! As you stand strong in faith during times of adversity, scripture says that you are achieving an eternal glory. When you confess your trust and reliance on God, you are passing the test.

If you are in the middle of tough times today, look to Jesus! The Bible says that He is the Author and Finisher of your faith. He is the one who writes faith on your heart and then develops it to completion on the inside of you. Your responsibility is to open your heart and choose words of faith and victory. Grow in faith and grow in character. Simply say a prayer as such during these times beloved:

Heavenly Father, thank You for working Your eternal glory in me. I cast my cares on You, knowing that my trials and troubles are only temporary. Thank You for Your eternal blessing on my life today and always in Jesus' name. Amen.

If you can pray this prayer during these moments of temporary hardship it exemplifies growth in your faith and reliance on His methods. And I believe these moments please God more than when we think we've arrived or believe we don't need His help. For this reason the Bible says that when we're weak, we are strong. The Apostle Paul in 2 Corinthians 12:10 (NIV) say it better. He said *...that is why, for Christ's sake, I delight in weaknesses, in insults, in hardships, in persecutions, in*

difficulties. For when I am weak, then I am strong.

It grieves God when we don't become who we're supposed to become. I will discuss this further in the next chapter however consider the chair, such as the one that is on the front cover. We all understand that chairs were built to be sat on but imagine if you had never seen one before. How would you know what it was designed for? The answer is that you would have to go the creator of the chair to determine the intended purpose of the chair. Likewise our purpose can only truly be determined by our Creator. Therefore stop allowing the opinions of others to trip you up because God had a purpose for your life way before anyone ever had an opinion about your life.

Also remember this; nothing can drag you down unless you are holding on to it. In order to get to where you want to be, you must be willing to let go of the things and people that are going in the wrong direction. You must be willing to let go of what God says is not for you and leave where you are. You are NOT stuck where you are unless you decide to be! Come on shake it off and get moving you got places to go and people to bless!

CHAPTER 2

<u>Processed for His Purpose</u>

Don't allow your process to be longer than God's process. I will discuss this on two levels because I'm speaking to the godly "leader" as well as to whom we would normally call the lay person/normal follower or church going saint. *Everything* that God does include process. However, sometimes His process is not carried out correctly as to the letter of the law, ***His*** *law mind you*, or intent of His purpose.

The general thought that is normally discussed regarding this subject in "the church" is going before God's timing or doing something before your time. But the flip side of the coin is in my opinion even more damaging. Because when you delay God's command or intent you shift not only the purpose of the thing or person that God is trying to utilize. You're shifting your position in the Kingdom as well because God doesn't want to share His glory with anyone, not even you. And what God demands from His most prized leaders in strategic places all over the world is obedience. ***Never put a question mark where God has put a period.***

[But I trust in you, O Lord; I say, "You are my God. My times are in your hand. Psalm 31:14-15]

There is process in everything. From the beginning of time to the minute that you're reading this book was and is a process. You weren't born with the ability to read; however, today you're able to read this book in its entirety. Everything that we see as well as don't see is in process right now. And every little process correlates to a bigger more meaningful process.

The trees are in the process of growing or dying, depending on how firm and fresh its roots have been planted and the level of sustainment that it regularly receives from its habitation. Also we have to consider how long it's been living as well as how long God has purposed for the tree to exist in its particular habitation. The wind even though we can't see it has been processed. Wind is comprised of H2O and is nothing but processed water. Plants release water through pores in their leaves. The evaporative loss of this water is called transpiration. Studies have revealed that about 10 percent of the moisture found in the atmosphere is released by plants through transpiration. The remaining 90 percent is mainly supplied by evaporation from oceans, seas, and other bodies of water (lakes, rivers, streams).

Transpiration is the process by which moisture is carried through plants from roots to small pores on the underside of leaves, where it changes to vapor and is released to the atmosphere. Transpiration is essentially evaporation of water from plant leaves.

Water is by far the most important substance on Earth. Water covers over 70 percent of the planet and makes up between 50 and 75 percent of the human body. In fact, it's one of the only things that we are positive, needs to be present for life to exist. When scientists look for life in our solar system and on exoplanets, they are looking for liquid water.

You might be asking yourself, why did he just go through all of that? The reason why I took the time to break some of God's natural processes down for you is to demonstrate that there are so many extremely important things going on at all times that have been set on its course by El Shaddai, God Almighty, and without these continual processes that are all inter-related and dependent upon each other; none of it or us would exist.

Your purpose is a lot like Transpiration, there are many forms that your process will carry you through that have been designed to produce an anointing for your specific purpose. H2O in all of its various forms, water, wind, ice, and vapor is still comprised of H2O. You will find yourself going down a lot of different roads at different intervals in your life and the whole time every road and obstacle is simply leading you to your purpose. The genius is that your purpose never changes. Why does it never change you ask? Because before you were formed in your mother's womb God knew you and pre-ordained your purpose – refer to Jeremiah 1:5.

The fact that the 44th President of the United States, Barak Obama, was a cub scout and used alcohol, marijuana, and cocaine during his teenage years; never altered the fact that God's ultimate purpose was for him to become the most powerful man on the face of the earth when his purpose finally reached its maturation. He is currently the most polished politician and speaker in the world and he admittedly states about his upbringing in Honolulu, Hawaii; "The opportunity that

Hawaii offered—to experience a variety of cultures in a climate of mutual respect—became an integral part of my world view, and a basis for the values that I hold most dear." He's basically highlighting the fact that some of the things he has done and some of the routes that his life has taken him through were not easy and all of the time "positive", however it was all necessary to become the man that he is today.

We should all take a cue from our current president in a spiritual sense and embrace everything that has brought you to the point of you reading this book right now. You're reading this kind of book because you want to do better, you want to be better. You knew that this book would equip you with even a little more ammunition to fight against the devil.

The devil will always bring up your past because he has no control over your future. So don't allow him to make you insecure about who you are in God as a man or a woman. We can't lead others if we're insecure or feeling inferior to everyone else. I know that you've been through hell beloved. But as Kimberly Jones, a preacher of faith, and founder of Conquering Hell in High Heels, has written; **the greatest thing about going through Hell is that you come out on fire!** You come out it with an extra spiritual endowment or anointing so respect it.

Let me show you someone who was careless and didn't have respect for his anointing:

Genesis 25

29 And Jacob boiled pottage; and Esau came from the field, and he was faint.

30 And Esau said to Jacob, "Feed me, I pray thee, with that same red

pottage, for I am faint"; therefore was his name called Edom.

31 And Jacob said, "Sell me this day thy birthright."

32 And Esau said, "Behold, I am at the point of dying. And what profit shall this birthright be to me?"

33 And Jacob said, "Swear to me this day." And he swore unto him, and he sold his birthright unto Jacob.

34 Then Jacob gave Esau bread and pottage of lentils; and he ate and drank, and rose up and went his way. Thus Esau despised his birthright.

Whatever you respect, you will protect! Don't, like Esau, sell your anointing and position in God for instant gratitude and cheap temporary thrills. The primary thing that separates good leaders from the average is vision. A person with vision will always focus on things in the long run, or what is commonly called the "big picture." Place your hope in things eternal beloved! Heaven is counting on you.

Respect YOUR anointing dear one! God has blessed all of us (believers) with a measure of the anointing in the same way that we have all been blessed with a measure of faith. Your ability to tap into the power of God depends on your ability to live a consecrated, holy, and pure life full of faith and the fruit to prove it. Esau was the first born and was the next in line after Isaac to lead the family into the future. He gave it up for a stew. He literally said to himself what does my title and position mean to anybody? I'm not going to act my age. I'm not going to show the maturity that I'm supposed to be showing. All I want is what I want and I want to satisfy myself now! All of this is basically what Esau did. He couldn't endure a little bit of pain that would eventually be satisfied anyway. Pain is a good indicator of the fact that you are on God's ordained path for your life. No pain, no gain!

God had already prophesized that he would wind up serving his YOUNGER brother. And we understand that God had selected in this way because he knew that Esau didn't have the CHARACTER that was necessary to fulfill the esteemed position and ultimately God's purpose. Esau was the bigger stronger brother who could hunt etc. but God showed Esau and all of us that He doesn't judge by the outside, He judges by what's on your inside. What's on your inside? Are your secret motives, thoughts, and desires pleasing to God?

To anoint means to smear or rub with oil. The Old Testament definition meant to apply or pour oil upon a person or even an object.
Old Testament example:
Psalms 92:10 says "But Thou has exalted my horn like that of the wild ox; I have been anointed with fresh oil."
New Testament example:
Acts 10:38 reads as such "...God anointed Jesus of Nazareth with the Holy Spirit and with power, who went about doing good and healing all who were oppressed by the devil, for God was with Him!"

God had ordained that Jacob and Esau would produce nations and trust assured that He has ordained something special to come out of your life. Get closer to God and deepen your relationship with Him to determine your purpose. The supernatural enablement that He has giving you is to be used for the Kingdom. Only you have it in the way that you have it. Don't disrespect the giver of your gifts by not using them and by not protecting them as something valuable. You must PROTECT your anointing because your purpose is contained within!

CHAPTER 3

The Cloud and the Fire

Beloved we are being divinely taken care of on so many levels that it's not funny. I want to relay a story from Numbers chapter 9 that will explain everything that I want to say on this subject.

Numbers 9:15-23 *[15] On the day the tabernacle, the tent of the covenant law, was set up, the cloud covered it. From evening till morning the cloud above the tabernacle looked like fire. [16] That is how it continued to be; the cloud covered it, and at night it looked like fire. [17] Whenever the cloud lifted from above the tent, the Israelites set out; wherever the cloud settled, the Israelites encamped. [18] At the LORD's command the Israelites set out, and at his command they encamped. As long as the cloud stayed over the tabernacle, they remained in camp. [19] When the cloud remained over the tabernacle a long time, the Israelites obeyed the LORD's order and did not set out. [20] Sometimes the cloud was over the tabernacle only a few days; at the LORD's command they would encamp, and then at his command they would set out. [21] Sometimes the cloud stayed only from evening till morning, and when it lifted in the morning, they set out. Whether by day or by night, whenever the cloud lifted, they set out. [22] Whether the cloud stayed over the tabernacle for two days or a month or a year, the Israelites would remain in camp and not set out; but when it lifted, they would set out. ²³ At the LORD's command they encamped, and at the LORD's command they set out. They obeyed the LORD's order, in accordance with his command through Moses.*

God used the elements that he created as signals for His people. When the cloud stayed still and settled they would stay put and set up camp. When it moved or lifted this was their signal to pack up and move their camp. It didn't matter how long or short the cloud had stayed. It was God's divine signal to them that they were to obey if they were to survive. The Cloud was God's Divine Protection from many things: The Sun, Sun Stroke, Sun Cancer, The Heat, Excessive Thirst, Dehydration etc. As a Soldier I know that one of the biggest enemies to our combat Soldiers that are and have served in any combat zone whether it was Europe, Germany, the Philippines, Vietnam or the Middle East are the elements. Spending days, weeks, and months in a desert is different than spending the same amount of time in a cultivated city. Existing in jungle like conditions takes much more skill than living in any of our modern cities.

Deserts have very little rainfall in a year, usually less than 10 inches (25 cm). Because there is very little moisture in the air to hold onto the heat from the hot days and desert nights tend to be very cold. Taken together, the extreme temperature fluctuations and lack of water make the desert environment a very harsh one in which to live. The plants and animals you will find there have a wide variety of special features that allow them to cope with desert conditions. Such as the cactus that retains water but have the hard exterior that protects it from the heat. And just like the cactus my brother and sister I want to let you know that you can go through your wilderness experience because you have been especially designed to withstand the elements. Somebody need to shout right there!

Some of you should've been dead seven years ago but because God was on your side. Listen to me somebody. Because God was on your side! Because GOD was on your side was the only reason that you made it through. I know He's the only reason why I am still here. I'm here because God graced me to be here and He has a purpose for me. I have to be real at this point because we can only be loosed by truth. It's amazing what God will do if we shut up. God was God before YOU got here, therefore let God be God. Translation ~ God doesn't need your help. However, He expects you to show everyone the same love and grace that He showed you to "woo" you into the Kingdom. Stay real and love on somebody tonight. Love on somebody tomorrow. God will take a murderer and make him a minister! He will take a sinner and transform him into a saint! He'll take the stripper and make her an Evangelist! But we got to stop acting like we're everybody's police and just be the example and speak His truths and let the Word "do what it do." God bless you beloved. I just want to love on everyone so much that they have to change! God died for me while I was yet a sinner because He loves me, He loves YOU and I Love you too. Let's go on.

So the cloud brought natural moisture because the very substance of clouds is gaseous moisture. This provided the dew in the morning and any other water necessary *in the middle of the desert beloved.* Truly amazing stuff.

The Bible tells us that the Israelites literally stayed in their "wilderness" for forty years without their clothes being singed and shoes wearing out; neither was their essence diminished. The Fire was their Natural Lighting System, because the wilderness is not the jungle that has a lot of trees and the sort that could be used to produce torches and light. It also kept away the wilderness animals such as the snakes, scorpions, lizards, mountain lions, as well as human enemies. A huge spiritual fire is a daunting barrier to someone who would want to wreak havoc on an unsuspecting group of people.

But God works according to The Law of Timing even though He Himself is not regulated by time He chooses to abide by the natural laws and systems that He's set in place. His queue for you to move in faith may invariably be different than the what is normal though beloved so remain flexible.

Read Numbers 9:17-18 ~*17 Whenever the cloud lifted from above the tent, the Israelites set out; wherever the cloud settled, the Israelites encamped. 18 At the LORD's command the Israelites set out, and at his command they encamped. As long as the cloud stayed over the tabernacle, they remained in camp.* God's people had no way of knowing whether they would camp in a specific location for a few days or a few years. They couldn't slip into a rut and trust in a schedule; they had to remain flexible. They learned to trust God, their ultimate leader. Therefore don't get complacent in the place that you're in because you might have to pack up quick and move out. If you are really an obedient soldier for the Lord you have to remember that He's our leader and He has things in store for us that we don't even know or understand. We have to get there His way though because He has to get all of the credit. If you get somewhere all on your own, I would say to you look around and ask God are you in His will. He'll talk to you beloved.

Numbers 9:23 *At the LORD's command they encamped, and at the LORD's command they set out. They obeyed the LORD's order, in accordance with his command through Moses.*

Wait for God's command beloved! Don't be impatient. Your impatience can kill your dream and destiny. Don't move on man's command. Move on **God's** Command! *Isaiah 40:31- They that wait on the Lord shall renew their strength. They shall mount up on wings of eagles. They shall run and not grow weary, they shall walk and not faint.*

You find out what God wants by listening to the heart of God. Listen to this. *And you will seek Me and find Me, when you search for me with all of your heart. Jeremiah 29:13.* God looks at you heart beloved. Every one of you that has spent a small fortune on putting letters behind your name in an attempt at self validation or otherwise, I got news for you. It doesn't impress God. I'm not downing education and higher education, I have a Masters Degree myself and working on a Doctor of Ministry as I'm in the process of writing this particular book, however I study to show *myself* approved. I'm not doing it to make myself feel better about me or to make others accept me. I have been high and I've been very low and God reminds me that He is sovereign and that the seasons of my life is in His hands and this fact keeps me very humble.

God isn't impressed by any of the things that would impress someone operating in a carnal mind. The only thing that moves God is our faith. The Bible says that without faith it's impossible to please God. We have to remember that. You're looking for a change in your finances? Then pray in faith to God and He'll supply your needs. According to Philippians 4:19; God says that He will supply all of our needs according to His riches and glory. But remember that God doesn't respond to your need, He responds to your Faith! However we have to give our Faith "focus."

Giving your faith focus means that you are specific in your request concerning that thing before God. Too many times we go to God with laundry lists of wants that we think are needs and never really pray for the most important thing. We have to learn how to keep the main thing the main thing. So many times we are majoring in the minor and magnifying the thing of the least importance. I've learned that God wants us to come to Him in a particular way, that's why He created His temple with one entrance.

Exodus 26:36a You shall make a screen for the door of the tabernacle. In God's Temple there is only one door! That means you can only access Him one way. Meaning you can only come to God on God's terms, so get over your self.

Refer to Numbers 10:11-28

[11] On the twentieth day of the second month of the second year, the cloud lifted from above the tabernacle of the covenant law. [12] Then the Israelites set out from the Desert of Sinai and traveled from place to place until the cloud came to rest in the Desert of Paran. [13] They set out, this first time, at the LORD's command through Moses.

[14] The divisions of the camp of Judah went first, under their standard. Nahshon son of Amminadab was in command. [15] Nethanel son of Zuar was over the division of the tribe of Issachar, [16] and Eliab son of Helon was over the division of the tribe of Zebulun. [17] Then the tabernacle was taken down, and the Gershonites and Merarites, who carried it, set out.

[18] The divisions of the camp of Reuben went next, under their standard. Elizur son of Shedeur was in command. [19] Shelumiel son of Zurishaddai was over the division of the tribe of Simeon, [20] and Eliasaph son of Deuel was over the division of the tribe of Gad. [21] Then the

Kohathites set out, carrying the holy things. The tabernacle was to be set up before they arrived.
²² The divisions of the camp of Ephraim went next, under their standard. Elishama son of Ammihud was in command.²³ Gamaliel son of Pedahzur was over the division of the tribe of Manasseh, ²⁴ and Abidan son of Gideoni was over the division of the tribe of Benjamin.
²⁵ Finally, as the rear guard for all the units, the divisions of the camp of Dan set out under their standard. Ahiezer son of Ammishaddai was in command. ²⁶ Pagiel son of Okran was over the division of the tribe of Asher, ²⁷ and Ahira son of Enan was over the division of the tribe of Naphtali. ²⁸ This was the order of march for the Israelite divisions as they set out.

From the preceding verses and many more it would be very clear that God has an order beloved. Confusion is not of God. Whenever God steps on the scene all disorder has to get in order. Void becomes earth. The earth produces trees, grass, and contains water. The waters have to stay in their place. And there are so many more examples. If you find that you're the type of person that has a problem with order, such as things like having patience; in the line at the grocery store, in traffic on the highway, in waiting for your husband to make a decision wives, or in waiting for your wife to finish shopping for that perfect dress or blouse before she releases you from her side men. Then it's something that you have to be honest with yourself about and realize that you will never be as complete and at peace as you can become without possessing this tangible trait. Allow everything that you've been through to teach you that it was only a matter of God's timing. Learn the art of patience in God so that you can discover Jehovah Shalom, the God of peace.

Alright, now let's look at the wisdom of Moses in *Numbers 10:29-32* ~
²⁹ Now Moses said to Hobab son of Reuel the Midianite, Moses' father-in-law, "We are setting out for the place about which the LORD said, 'I will give it to you.' Come with us and we will treat you well, for

the LORD has promised good things to Israel."
³⁰ He answered, "No, I will not go; I am going back to my own land and my own people."
³¹ But Moses said, "Please do not leave us. You know where we should camp in the wilderness, and you can be our eyes.³² If you come with us, we will share with you whatever good things the LORD gives us."

He understood the following concept: You can't lead someone somewhere you've never been. You can't instruct or convict someone in an area that you're not doing or qualified yourself. Never allow anyone to mentor you in an area that they're not qualified or have operated in. Tell them thanks but no thanks. Again, you can't lead anybody somewhere you haven't been.

Next thing Moses did is that he let the "Ark" which we can use the phrase "presence of God" go before him and the people on a daily. *³³ So they set out from the mountain of the Lord and traveled for three days. The ark of the covenant of the Lord went before them during those three days to find them a place to rest.³⁴ The cloud of the Lord was over them by day when they set out from the camp.*

We have to let the Presence of God go before us every day. Let the presence of God in your life do the speaking for you. We make the mistake of sending out our own spirit; our own intellect, our own ideas. But God has given us the key to victorious living many times over in His Word. Please consider what I'm explaining to you concerning Moses and the way he led God's people through their wilderness experience. I'll recount the important steps again for you:

1. Moses sought the Lord. Meaning he had a relationship with God. (Numbers 10:13)

2. He waited for God's signal. (Numbers 10:13;28)

3. He and all of the people were prepared **before** God gave them any signal. Whether it was to move or stay put. (Numbers 10:33)

4. He kept his humility and utilized wisdom by keeping the right people on board in their proper places. As he did with his father-in-law. (Numbers 10:29)

5. He let the Ark, or Presence of God, go before him. Meaning he didn't go in his own strength.

6. Finally he decreed and declared the blessings over him and the people every single day and night. Consider verses 35 and 36:

^{35} Whenever the ark set out, Moses said, "Rise up, LORD! May your enemies be scattered; may your foes flee before you."
^{36} Whenever it came to rest, he said, "Return, LORD, to the countless thousands of Israel."

Beloved every since God gave me this revelation in the Word regarding using the power of the Holy Spirit and sending Him out before we even embark on our daily journeys, I've been decreeing and declaring these same scriptures every morning and so should you if you want to see radical and victorious change in your life.

DAILY DECLARATION

Rise up oh Lord, may your enemies be scattered; may your foes flee before you.

I declare even my enemies shall bless me. I have favor with God and man. Me and my house shall serve the Lord!

Halleluiah! I just gave some of you the keys that you've needed to find your whole lives. I believe that as you utilize this knowledge your life will never be the same. Remember this also; **Good Success is in Your Mouth:**

Joshua 1:8 - This Book of the Law shall not depart from your mouth, but you shall meditate in it day and night… For then you will make your way prosperous, and then you will have good success.

I had always wondered why the Torah (the first five books of Moses) is read out loud by the Jews. Then, I learned from a Jewish Christian that for generations, they read God's Word out loud because of Joshua 1:8 — "This Book of the Law shall not depart from your mouth, but you shall meditate in it day and night…"

The word "meditate" in English means to ponder. But in Hebrew, it is the word **hagah**, which means *to utter or mutter under your breath*. In other words, when you meditate on God's Word, you speak forth or confess His Word instead of just giving it mental assent.

My friend, hagah God's Word by confessing verses in the areas that you are believing God for breakthrough. Confess verses like, "Honor the Lord with your possessions, and with the first fruits of all your increase; so your barns will be filled with plenty…" (Proverbs 3:9 –10) And watch God bless you! Your way will be made prosperous and you will enjoy good success.

"Pastor, I am waiting for God to make my way prosperous."

No, the Bible says that you will make your way prosperous when you hagah God's Word. So speak forth verses in the areas which you want to see breakthroughs and you will have good success.

Some people have success that destroys them. You don't see them in church anymore and their family members don't get to see them either. That is bad success. But when you hagah God's Word, you will have good success that does not destroy you.

Now, confessing God's Word does not move God to do things for you. It is not a formula. God had already moved when He gave up Jesus to die for you. **However, when you confess His Word, it moves you from a position of doubt to faith**. It moves your heart from a position of "Is it true?" to "I believe it!" When that happens, "you will make your way prosperous, and then you will have good success!" *Therefore never be scared to strive for your greater purpose, because if you're afraid to fail you don't even deserve the prosperity of God and good success.*

Points to remember:

/ If you don't have the heart of God you'll start criticizing and complaining. God HATES complainers and complaining. Refer to *Numbers 11:1 Now the people complained in the hearing of the Lord;* **and when He heard it His wrath flared up so that the fire of the Lord burned among them and consumed the outskirts of the camp.**

// Verse 1 of Numbers 11 said when God **heard** it. Don't allow your disappointments to show. You can disagree without being disagreeable. Never let them **see** you sweat!

/// Verse 2. *But when the people cried out to Moses, he prayed to the Lord and the fire died out.* Don't take the Goodness of God for granted.

BE THANKFUL!

//// Verse 3. *Hence that place was called Taberah, because there the fire of the Lord burned among them.* We all have a TABERAH place in our life. Don't forget the things you have gone through because those experiences are the seeds that fertilize your growth. So remember where you came from but be sure to not worship your past because when you reflect on your past to the point of obsession it becomes worship and you'll always remain there. Move forward.

Don't let the disrespect of people cause you to act out of character. God will fight your battles. God spared the people due to the prayer life and relationship that He had with Moses. Never get this part twisted, God is **always** in control. Keep your relationship with God and His men and women right and you're life will be full of God's favor. It will be to the point where other people will be jealous and say it's not fair. But God's favor ain't fair.

Finally, if you don't like critics, don't be one!

CHAPTER 4

<u>H</u>idden <u>W</u>isdom

You cannot make the right decision with wrong information.

Dr. Mike Murdoch

Beloved, one of the most overlooked groups of scriptures in the Bible is contained in 1 Corinthians 2. In verse 5-8 Paul tells us that *[5] that your faith should not be in the wisdom of men but in the power of God. [6] However, we speak wisdom among those who are mature, yet not the wisdom of this age, nor of the rulers of this age, who are coming to nothing. [7] But we speak the wisdom of God in a mystery, the hidden wisdom which God ordained before the ages for our glory, [8] which none of the rulers of this age knew; for had they known, they would not have crucified the Lord of glory.*

My disclaimer up front about this chapter is that it'll be the longest in this book and it contains some truth and hidden wisdom for some of you and just a revisit of information that others probably already know. If you are like the religious heretics of Jesus' age who were leaders mind you, you'll probably want to skip just this chapter and read the rest of the book because this chapter will stretch your thinking and even offend some of you in order to allow for spiritual growth to occur in your life not to mention add wisdom.

The most elusive thing that most humans live their whole lives without discovering is their purpose. It is the most elusive and in turn can be the single most disappointing aspect to never fully realize until it's too late in a person's life. The ability to know and understand your purpose is so precious that many of us would or have already willingly sold our souls to something other than God for the knowledge.

Since the Garden of Eden to now humans have been longing for a way to know what tomorrow will bring before tomorrow. From the serpent in the garden (Gen. 2:17) to the witch or wizard to the trusted soothsayer advisors of the Assyrians over 5000 years ago to the gypsy, to the psychic/ fortuneteller it is definitely one of the oldest tools and tactics used by the Kingdom of Darkness since man's beginning.

The tool and tactic that I'm referring too in the previous paragraph is that of playing on men and woman's desire to "know" the future, specifically their future. Many men and women have paid top dollars and have sold their soul literally to Satan just for a glimpse of what will happen in the future, what they will become and for even a glimpse of why they are here.

I was so shocked in 2005 when my brigade, the 56th Stryker Brigade was sent to Louisiana for disaster relief efforts due to the infamous Hurricane Katrina. At one point we moved further into the water torn city and I was appalled that the few businesses that remained open despite not having consistent flowing electricity and clean water and even more atrocious circumstances were the strip clubs and the numerous fortune teller businesses that inhabit Louisiana, especially New Orleans.

I had to pull my unit aside and admonish them because of some of their illicit behavior, telling them to think of how these young women in these clubs are washing themselves (without clean running water mind you) and the spirit that's driving their kind of business especially in such a catastrophic for all of them. And I even went so far as to explain that there was a chief demon of lust, and I knew his name, of which I will explain in the next paragraph, waiting at the doors of the big Larry Flynn strip club that was right on Bourbon street and the many smaller ones. I had to tell them that he was waiting for them. I could feel him even when I walked across the street from it. All of my unit respected my wishes and did not enter any of these places; at least not while they were with me. Funny stuff.

That of which I write in the next paragraph are only for those who feel they have been called to the work of the *Deliverance ministry* and those who have a desire to understand more of the *principalities, powers, and rulers of darkness, and spiritual wickedness in in high places* from Ephesians 6:12. It will expand your mind and enlighten you to a point that you will be dangerous at least on this specific topic that we're discussing right now and will cause you to become a target of the Kingdom of satan because you will have knowledge that will *approve* you to cast them out. If you don't want this level of spiritual warfare skip to the next chapter, it's okay. No one will know except you, the demons who are watching and recording all of your actions just like the angels in heaven, and of course God.

To be a wise person and leader you must keep yourself exposed to as many diverse sources of information as possible. ~ Pastor Rick Warren

----

The only Gospel that I will ever preach is that of Jesus Christ. The only book that I want you to believe without question is the Bible. Consider Galatians 1:8-9: 8) *But though we, or an angel from heaven, preach any other gospel unto you than that which we have preached unto you, let him be accursed. 9) As we said before, so I say now again, if any man preach any other gospel unto you than that ye have received, let him be accursed.* **So please understand that the next few pages are for your information only to stretch you and to get rid of ignorance, not to teach you another doctrine. The only doctrine you need is JESUS!**

Paul and all of the Apostles taught from the whole body of work to include even some non-canonical books; however again I *only* preach Jesus and the next thing that I'll enlighten you is from some of the non-canonical sources that they were taught by every religious leader during their time. In fact, 2 Timothy 3:16 says ~ *All scripture is given by inspiration of God, and is profitable for doctrine, for reproof, for correction, for instruction in righteousness:* However it's important to note that Paul wasn't only referring to what we widely consider as the unalterable Word of God, the canonized Bible. He was referring to all of the sacred literature that were commonly circulated during those days. Now that I've got that out of the way, let me educate you. Consider the next insight that God allows us to understand once again and then I'll explain further about the ancient demon of lust.

"For we wrestle not against flesh and blood, but against principalities, against powers, against the rulers of the darkness of this world, against spiritual wickedness in high places," Ephesians 6:12.

Those principalities that are referred to in Ephesians 6 would love nothing more than to water down our knowledge of the things of God and of spiritual matters which is why in Revelations 22 it is written:

[18] For I testify unto every man that heareth the words of the prophecy of this book, If any man shall add unto these things, God shall add unto him the plagues that are written in this book:

[19] And if any man shall take away from the words of the book of this prophecy, God shall take away his part out of the book of life, and out of the holy city, and from the things which are written in this book.

[20] He which testifieth these things saith, Surely I come quickly. Amen. Even so, come, Lord Jesus.

[21] The grace of our Lord Jesus Christ be with you all. Amen.

It is my intent as a teacher to not allow this device of satan to work, hence the next information is for the normal Christian who hasn't heard any other information other than what would traditionally come from a Sunday morning pulpit. After the next few pages I'll take you back to the mainstream teachings.

The only recorded name of the aforementioned demon of lust is asmodeus or asmodai (Hebrew: אשמדאי *ashmedai*). He is "a" king of demons mostly known from the deuterocanonical *Book of Tobit*, in which he is the primary antagonist. The book of Tobit was deemed canonical by the Alexandrian Jews and the Palestinian Jews and was canonized at the Council of Trent in 39 AD. A Hebrew and Aramaic version of this book was found with the Dead Sea Scrolls in 1947.

The same demon is also mentioned in some Talmudic legends, for instance, in the story of the construction of the Temple of Solomon. He was supposed by some Renaissance Christians to be the King of the Nine Hells. He also is referred to as one of the seven princes of Hell. In Binsfeld's classification of demons, each one of these princes represents one of the seven deadly sins (Pride, Lust, Envy, Sloth, Greed, Gluttony, and Wrath). You're asking yourself right now is there Princes in satan's Kingdom. I assure you there are. That's why Eph. 6:12 uses the word "principalities" because there is a prince over every heavenly (first and second heaven) territory. Remember only God is omnipresent. satan is not and so he had to form a government that will equip him to "act" as if he's everywhere and inflict his influence.

This lust demon is therefore responsible for twisting people's sexual desires. He is characterized by the influencing of carnal desires and it is said that people who fall to asmodeus' ways will be sentenced to an eternity in the second level of hell.

Now I went so far as to "go there" regarding the name and function of this particular demon because when you have knowledge and understanding of a particular thing in the spirit world and **believe** it, you gain the understanding and therefore the ability to speak directly to it and the wisdom and power to resist it as well as cast it away. *And these signs shall follow them that **believe**; In my name shall they cast out devils; they shall speak with new tongues; Mark 16:17.* Whose name do we cast out any demon beloved? That's right, His name is

Jesus! Therefore use His name and do not fear.

Another reason why I brought up this particular subject is because I started this book discussing about how a lot of human beings have done and are doing many things to find out their future and/or purpose in this life and I would like to submit to someone reading this book that this is due to a lust problem more than anything else. The Bible says that we are drawn away by the **lust** of **our own** flesh. Consider James chapter 1:

***12)** Blessed is the man that endureth temptation: for when he is tried, he shall receive the crown of life, which the Lord hath promised to them that love him. **13)** Let no man say when he is tempted, I am tempted of God: for God cannot be tempted with evil, neither tempteth he any man: **14)** But every man is tempted, when he is drawn away of his own lust, and enticed.*

The Bible tells us specifically that it is our **own lust** that will get us in trouble. Not some foreign totally unrelated lust that will do us in. There are other types of lust other than sexual. Whatever we secretly desire and are craving for to the point of obsession, envy, and jealousy are some of things that eventually turns into lust that can be all consuming and severely fatal. The lust of success and power are so prevalent amongst so many "ambitious Christians" of our generation and it is drawing them away from the authentic works of Christ that they have been called to.

I'll tell you two more short stories that lust or asmodeus is normally included in to illustrate this point. NOT to get you to believe the story because the story comes from a non-canonical source and I know that my books are to main stream Protestant/ Charismatic/ Pentecostal/

Evangelical/ Orthodox Christian Believers. However, I want to ensure that you're edified and have learned something you never knew by the reading of this book and would inform you that most serious seminary students, scholars, catholic priests, historians and those who have studied to show themselves approved have knowledge of these texts and stories. So why shouldn't you?

Also, one of the underlying reasons that a lot of sacred books that were commonly read and accepted before the Council of Trent in 1546 and Biblical Canonization really took place were rejected from inclusion into the Bible because of the discussion of angels and demons (fallen angels) and their names and stories that included human involvement in spiritual warfare. Ask yourself is that helpful to the body of Christ or a hindrance? The answer is that it's both. A lot of individuals would make doctrines out of the spiritual beings discussed in the works almost in the same way that Catholics pretty much pray to and worship the "Virgin Mary." Or how Jehovah Witness and the Watchtower Society believe that Jesus and the Ark Angel Michael are one in the same. I'm so glad that it says in Proverbs 21:30 that "There is no human wisdom or understanding or counsel that can prevail against the Lord." I know that I'm presenting a lot of new information to some of you but let's dig a little deeper.

At one point all of the texts and information I'm discussing were normal scriptures to be spoken about and taught on in Christian/ Judean/ and Catholic fellowships all over the world. Let me repeat one scripture and state another to really get it into your system and keep you focused before I move on through this chapter.

2 Timothy 2:15 ~ Study to shew thyself approved unto God, a workman that needeth not to be ashamed, rightly dividing the word of truth.

*2 Timothy 3:16 ~ **All** scripture is given by inspiration of God, and is profitable for doctrine, for reproof, for correction, for instruction in righteousness:*

The first of the two short stories that I'll relate to you real fast includes the Angel Raphael. Now again I have to stop and educate the reader. Raphael is commonly accepted as one of the Ark-Angels and even one of the Seven Angels who stand before God with seven trumpets of Revelations 8:2 with Michael and Gabriel but most untrained Christians don't realize that his name will not be found in the canonized Bible. His name is only found in several Jewish apocryphal books and his name means "It is God who heals". The other four names of the angels can be found there as well. Not to stray from the subject but I can give you about 20 more truths that we teach and discuss in the deeper things of God as doctrine which are not based in the canonized Bible. You would have to look at the Apocryphal books which are always contained in the Catholic Bibles and books of the sort.

Even Jesus Himself in Luke 11 taught from what we would consider the un-canonized Bible. After He had performed an exorcism of the mute boy He then came out of it and spoke to the masses and stated that the Queen of the South had come to King Solomon to enquire of his wisdom; however one greater than Solomon is here, referring to Himself. Sounds kind of strange that Jesus would speak of Solomon after an exorcism until you discover that it was taught in Jesus day that Solomon was not only the wisest man in regards to things in general but in regards to those things of the spirit world as well.

There is another book of Solomon written in the first person by

Solomon that isn't included in our traditional Bible. Did you know that beloved? It is written and said that he was given a ring that could cast out demons and wield demons and the texts even go so far to explain that he summoned demons to finish the building of the great Temple of Jerusalem. Jesus was saying that He had more wisdom than Solomon in terms of the things of the spirit. He was saying He had more knowledge of the angels and their operation in the spiritual and natural world than anyone because He was the Son of God and He and the Father are one! However, let's move on because I know this is blowing some of you away right now. In all of your getting get understanding beloved. The FULL council of the things of God is going to be taught again so that we won't miss the "signs" of His second coming.

The Word lets us know that in the last days men will preach "seducing doctrines" and what better way to seduce somebody than to OMIT those things that are true. People are perishing for lack of knowledge. Taking pills because they're fighting forces that they don't even **believe** exist. I was talking to a pastor one day regarding this kind of subject and asked him how can you cast out what you don't believe? Really it's so stupid and this is why Jesus had to pull his disciples away and give them all of the information. He taught them the secrets of the Kingdom of Heaven. Let me give you the rest of the story real fast before we get back to the safer teachings of the Bible. However, one more important repetition;

I warn everyone who hears the words of the prophecy of this book; If anyone adds anything to them, God will add to him the plagues described in this book. ~ Revelations 22:18

Was the prior scripture directed at us, meaning this generation alone? No it was to John the Beloved's own generation as well and probably more so because he knew that they were watering down the things of God and omitting the secrets and mysteries that Jesus turned a whole world upside down with. I know that some of you who are familiar with me are laughing right now. And trust me so am I. I want to go deeper but God is not releasing me too. I will say this however that the doctrine that the *Anti-Christ* will one day bring to the world will have hints of the truth which is why it will be so seducing and it wouldn't be seducing if we taught the whole council of the things of God.

In Matthew 24:24-25 Jesus said *For false Christs and false prophets will appear and perform great signs and miracles to deceive even the elect-if that were possible. See I have told you ahead of time.* The only thing that could deceive a real man or woman of God is something that has so much truth to it that it can't be argued against or proven incorrect. We're so far away from some of the ancient truths and teachings that this will be easy for him once he comes on the scene.

The asmodeus (lust) of the Book of Tobit is attracted to Sarah, Raguel's daughter, and is not willing to let any husband possess her (Tobit 6:13); hence he slays seven successive husbands on their wedding nights, impeding the sexual consummation of the marriages. When the young Tobias is about to marry her, asmodeus proposes the same fate for him, but Tobias is enabled or maybe a better word is empowered, through the counsels of his attendant angel Raphael, to render him innocuous, which means uninjured . By placing a fish's heart and liver on red-hot cinders, Tobias produces a smoky vapor that causes the demon to flee to Egypt, where Raphael binds him (Tobit 8:2-3).

First, why would I even bring this *story* up? I brought it up because it indicates that there are certain principalities and realms that certain demons cannot move in. In our churches we always read or hear Ephesians 6:12 but honestly most "Saints" (I'm going to talk more about "Saints" a little later) don't even understand what it means. The reason why I feel the need to use this story instead of a traditional one and the need to divulge more information than the normal Christian author is because God has told me that His people are operating without the power and knowledge that they are supposed to possess because satan has hidden, stolen, and destroyed the knowledge from their (our) minds. However, the devil is a liar and I reiterate that it is my every intention to expose him and his dirty little tactics!

If there is a certain person, place, city, state or country that you have traditionally always engaged in sin it could be because of the strongman (a k a ~ prince of that principality) and stronghold that rules over that particular person and/or place. Pay attention to your behavior and bind him!

"I will give you the keys of the kingdom of heaven; whatever you bind on earth will be bound in heaven, and whatever you loose on earth will be loosed in heaven." Matthew 16:19.

In this story Raphael wasn't able to bind the demon until he was over the province of Egypt. Some blessings and curses are geographical. Be cognizant of where you are and with whom at all times. That's why the institution of "church" and the "church age" is so important. By attending church daily, meaning at least weekly or two to three times a week you are keeping yourself girded up with the Word of God and developing the ability to use the spiritual weapons that He promised each of us at Salvation. That's why we are told to *forsake not the assembly of ourselves together.*

"*Church attendance is as vital to a disciple as a transfusion of rich, healthy blood to a sick man*". – Dwight L. Moody

However, be cognizant that we are moving out of the Church age into the Kingdom age but that topic is to be saved for another book.

I said that we should bind "him" a few paragraphs ago. I say him (them) because all angels are masculine, even though they can come in any form. Don't take the reference of your Friday night horror show or movie just refer to the Word of God where it lets us know that the angels were called the Sons of God.

Genesis 6: 1-4

[1] Now it came to pass, when men began to multiply on the face of the earth, and daughters were born to them, [2] that the sons of God saw the daughters of men, that they were beautiful; and they took wives for themselves of all whom they chose. [3] And the LORD said, "My Spirit shall not strive with man forever, for he is indeed flesh; yet his days shall be one hundred and twenty years." [4] There were giants on the earth in those days, and also afterward, when the sons of God came in to the daughters of men and they bore children to them. Those were the mighty men who were of old, men of renown.

I could go further with the explanation to show that all angels were masculine such as in Job 1 when all of the sons of God presented themselves before God and lucifer was in the midst and many more. But to be brief, the "woman" first and appearance and introduction to creation occurred when she was created on Earth and before that creation, females didn't exist. Women were specifically made for men. This creation was and is so awesome and beautiful that it not only has made the most powerful kings and nations go to war, change their laws, religions, and Gods. It has made heavenly beings leave their angelic realm and rightful place to *experience* them. Women, you are so special! Consider your worth!

Lastly, the demon of lust was never more apparent than in King Solomon. He dealt with an external lust of the flesh and an internal spiritual and emotional lust for power and **more.** Be careful of always wanting **more** beloved because more is not always what God has planned for your life. Learn to be content in whatever state you find yourself in and do the best with what you have.

It is said in the *Testament of Solomon*, a 1st–3rd century text, that he invokes fallen spirits (demons) to aid in the construction of the Temple. We recognize right away Solomon's desire to know more. His father David had a great prophet Nathan for the duration of his reign and life however Solomon did not develop the same relationship with God and the renowned holy men of God in the same way that his father did. Solomon, living in the blessings of David, tried to take care of most things on his own. The demon appears and predicts Solomon's kingdom will one day be divided (Testament of Solomon, verse 21–25). When Solomon interrogates asmodeus further, the king learns that asmodeus is thwarted by the angel Raphael who utilized the sheatfish of Assyria. And there is another story in this Apocryphal book that explains how asmodeus actually took Solomon's place for a period of time as Solomon was chasing the god's of his many wives and kept up a nightly regiment of going into Solomon's wives for years until he was found out. Simply amazing and mind altering things to think about I know. But I'm not saying you have to accept any of it beloved. But I do want you to have knowledge of these things and be aware.

The Jesus era church missed him at His first coming due to an error in their interpretation and knowledge of the plans and written Word of God. Let's not make the same mistake twice. A lot of those "holy" men during Jesus era are baking in hell right now because they couldn't stand somebody to come along and tell them that they were in error. They felt this so passionately that they killed the very one that they claimed to know so much about, revere, and worship. Lord, give us the eyes to see and the ears to hear! Increase our faith and help our unbelief!

Now let's get back to more mainstream teaching, concepts and ideas because God has given me a burden to reach the world as well as to prepare the **saints**.

Larry Edward Birchett, Jr.

CHAPTER 5

The Saint

Would you consider yourself a saint? After doing a study on the word Saint I found out that the Greek word for saint is *hagios*; which was normally used in first century Greek to mean "devoted to the gods" (the Greek idols), but in the New Testament, *hagios* mostly refers to persons and things that were connected to the true God who is in Heaven. A variant of hagios is *hagos* which translates into an awful thing. Isn't it funny that when you understand the context of a thing it can change your whole perception? It's almost like when we in our current day vernacular say "wow that car is bad" when what we really mean is that car is awesome! Will people one thousand years from now understand that? Or will they have to do a little research just like we're doing right now?

In the Old Testament, the singular form "saint" occurs only in Psalms 106:16 and Daniel 8:13, as a translation of the Hebrew adjective qadowsh (holy). 34 Old Testament passages contain the plural form "saints" (translated from the Hebrew qadowsh, qaddiysh or qodesh which referred to "holiness" or chaciyd which referred to faithfulness).

In the New Testament, the singular form "saint" is found in only one passage, Philippians 4:21, which say "salute every saint". It was translated from the Greek adjective hagios, "holy".

This floored me because I always thought of the saints of old as the real and authentic ones. At one time I believed that a saint was something to be almost revered; someone special and strong and beautiful with fire shooting out of their eyes with angels standing behind them. But I found out that even though the end result might be something to the magnitude of the exaggerated description of my previous thought concerning the subject, and I'm being a little humorous; the initial build up to that determination is dependant on the observer.

See, the saints, or "holy ones" (Greek tous hagious), were people that were set apart for God. Indeed, the meaning is that God had separated a number of people from this world, for himself and for his son Jesus.

The adjective hagios is found in 229 passages of the Greek text of the New Testament. Some of the instances are referred to the Holy Spirit, a few to God's holy angels, several passages to Jesus as the "Holy One", and then some referring to a "holy" place.

So it's good to know that the New Testament talks about 'saints' but the reality is that it's not always referring to the people of our day in the way that we use it. In Acts 9:13, for example, it talks about "the saints in Jerusalem" or that is "the holy ones in Jerusalem", referring to the people who had been set apart for God in that first century town. Therefore we could suppose that those are us that are truly in the process of sanctification can be considered saints. Those of us who are refusing to be changed and show *evidence* of this fact are not saints. So just because you sing the song 'Oh When the Saints Come Marching In' doesn't mean that you are one. Just because you go to church every Sunday with a lot of the *saints* doesn't mean that you can call yourself one unless you're showing the *evidence* of the grace of God in your life. And normally there is a little process to get to this point.

There is somebody who is reading this right now and doesn't agree. Let me say this to you, if you feel as though God had decided to use you whenever He first started using you because of your beauty, intellect, or righteousness you're either fully deceived and in denial because you're operating in a proud and abhorrent spirit. Or you are headed for a rude awakening. God only uses the humble. He resides with the humble and the contrite and we have to ensure that we don't get humility confused with performance, false humility, weakness, and insecurity.

The Wiklepedia definition of saint is "a holy person. In various religions, saints are people who are believed to have exceptional holiness." The Bible only shows one person that was expressly called a saint: "They envied Moses also in the camp, and Aaron the saint of the LORD." (Psalms 106:16-18). Now the word *saint* is also translated into the word "consecrated" for those who have the NIV version of the Bible. The Good News Translates the Hebrew word into the English word holy. Of which every saint is supposed to be and apparently is what Aaron was even though we know some of his shortcomings. Also to look a little further the apostle Paul declared himself to be "less than the least of all "saints" in Ephesians 3:8.

The earlier definition of *saint* being an awful thing relates to the God ordained process that one has to endure to really be considered a *saint*. It is not what the Catholic would consider as a requirement for sainthood and all of that garbage. It has nothing to do with works or the sort. Please refer to *Ephesians 2:8-10 For it is by grace you have been saved, through faith - and not from yourselves, it is the gift of God, not by works, so that no one can boast.*

For the life of me I will never understand why Catholics even waste their time on giving a title that can only be given by God Himself because only He knows who the true *saints* are. I especially don't like the posthumous awarding of religious titles to human beings for the purpose of reverence and worship to them because this honor is God's alone. If you can't tell me that I'm a good man now while I'm living then don't lie at my funeral and tell everybody that I was a good man. Just say what I am. But if my fruit is good then that means I was connected to the "good tree". What am I saying in short beloved? Don't pray to anybody in Heaven other than God. Pray to God in the name of Jesus always and you will never be disappointed. Some of the human beings that **we** think are going to be in Heaven won't and some of them that we think didn't make it in are there right now serving and enjoying God. I've told you the truth now discipline yourself and adhere to the ways of the Lord.

Discipline comes with preparation. You have to go through Basic Training before you can ever operate in the advance things of God. Let's talk about Basic Training.

"Discipline is the bridge between goals and accomplishment." -Jim Rohn

We live in a society where everyone wants to be an officer without first being the Private. When I went to the United States Army basic training in FT Jackson, SC they didn't even allow me to call myself a Soldier until I completed Basic Training. **You have to go through the process to appreciate the promise.** Why do we even feel as though we're worthy of extra rank or the higher grade when we know we haven't went through the necessary levels and preparation time? I often wonder why some individuals feel as though they can handle more responsibility when it is clear to me that they can barely handle what's on their plate at that moment. **God has four phases that he uses to prepare his Saints for Victorious Living:**

God Prepares You.

Gives You Direction

Allowing of Distractions

Expectation (Victorious Living)

Part of being *in process* is **preparation**. However, the realization that you are involved in something bigger than yourself, such as God's process, is most times accompanied by some sort of trigger. The trigger that most people recognize is pain. Pain let's you know that something not normal is happening and it's not until you come to this realization can the process properly start. An individual that is thrown in a furnace will first feel the effects of the fire. The heat, pain, smoke, different smell, different visual surroundings, mental signals being sent to every major part of your body; you ever wonder why when you're going through some of the most difficult times in your life you lose your appetite or food taste different? It's because of the fire. Welcome to the process.

Sometimes Preparation requires separation. And this separation can be you separating yourself from others or God removing others from you. Remember a translation of the word saint is *consecrated* therefore don't despise what God is doing in your life as He's maneuvering those in your circle and maybe even picking you up and relocating you to another place just so that He can have your undivided attention and teach you one on one. See I'm going to explain to you later that your promise is contained in a certain *place* not necessarily a certain time, but we'll get back to that because I have another example of preparation that I'd like to expose you too.

Consider the Spartan. When a baby boy was born to Spartan parents the father would take the baby to a council of elders, who would look over the child for any birth defects. If the council found the baby to be in quality condition to become a Spartan the baby was given back to his parents for six more years. At age seven the boy would be taken from his home and placed into a military training facility. At age twelve the boy would be removed from the military training facility and given nothing for one year, forcing him to learn how to survive on basic human instinct. From the ages of thirteen to twenty, when the Spartan would begin fighting, the child would play serious war "games" in preparation for the battles he would encounter in his future.

A lot of individuals in our generation have lost the respect of the preparation phase in anything including our military and spiritual leaders. We as the body of Christ have to refocus those who would hear and learn of the auspices of God to become better prepared to conduct the work of God. It is critical for the longevity of any minister or leader in Christendom.

The second phase is the Direction phase in which God will instruct you once you're ready. After the preparation comes the direction. But beware that as soon as God gives us direction the devil will come and try to distort the message and distract us which leads us into the third phase.

Our directions can come in many forms. God will sometimes speak to us through our dreams. That's why I have a dream journal. Every dream that I can remember is written down in this book to be reviewed because you are never more connected to the things of the spirit than when you're sleep. I explained in my first book, Reverence for the Storm, how in Genesis 42 God gave Pharaoh a warning dream that only Joseph could come and explain and interpret. The bottom line of the teaching of that particular story is that God speaks to all of us, Believers and Non-Believers and one prime method that He uses is our dreams. As I go through certain things in my life and I read the dreams that accompany these instance I'm learning how to interpret the message or dream language that God uses for me. Try it. It's totally awesome.

He speaks to us through our spiritual leaders. That's why we have to pray for our Apostles, Bishops, Prophets, Missionaries, Pastors, Elders, and those respected spiritual leaders that God has ordained to pour into us on a daily basis. They're God's mouthpieces and we have to listen for God's unique message to us. That's why He tells us to not forsake the assembly of ourselves together. Somewhere in the obedience of our congregating lie our answers for daily living. But if we never get into that spiritual and hallowed place of God's people we'll continually miss out.

God will send us angels, give us visions, send situations in our lives and we have to recognize that all of these things are **direction** beloved.

The third phase is the allowing of distractions. God will never tempt you but He'll allow the tempter to tempt you and He will allow your resolve and love for Him to be tested. You ever noticed that as soon as you made the switch in your mind that you're going to go after God with everything that you've got and that nothing will inhibit your obedience to Him, that that's the exact time when all hell broke out in your life?

I distinctly remember that when I made this decision that's when I went through some of the biggest tests in my life. This shouldn't come as a surprise to anybody because the Bible says in 2 Timothy 3:12 ~ Yea, and all that will live godly in Christ Jesus shall suffer persecution. But I don't think any of us expect it to come from our own. Sometimes the people closest to you are holding the knife that you're feeling in your back. But if we walk in knowledge of this possibility and the spirit behind some people we can protect our spirits when these attacks occur and keep ourselves encouraged.

The last Beatitude in the gospel of Matthew reads like this.
Matthew 5:10. Blessed are those who are persecuted for righteousness' sake, for theirs is the kingdom of heaven.
11 Blessed are you when they revile and persecute you, and say all kinds of evil against you falsely for My sake.
12 Rejoice and be exceedingly glad, for great is your reward in

heaven, for so they persecuted the prophets who were before you.

The blessing here is upon those that suffer. It is important to notice that here; we are not talking about suffering in a general sense. This is not about the suffering that you experience because you have cancer or because you lost your job. As Christians, God expects that we face these stressful situations in a spiritual and Christ like manner. But this is not the point of the Beatitude. The Lord Jesus is talking about a suffering that is peculiar to genuine believers: the suffering that is endured because of

righteousness. It is a suffering that only those who live godly lives experience; those who have righteousness in their lives.

Don't confuse what I'm discussing with suffering due to your own sinful conduct. God does not bless those who suffer because of their sinful conduct. Jesus is talking about a situation in which you suffer because of righteousness, and not for any other reason.

Now back to the distraction. In 1 Kings 13 God commanded a prophet, a real man of God to travel from Judah to Bethel to give a word against the false altars and fake priests that Jeroboam had set up there.

1 Kings 13
King James Version (KJV)
13 And, behold, there came a man of God out of Judah by the word of the LORD unto Bethel: and Jeroboam stood by the altar to burn incense.
² And he cried against the altar in the word of the LORD, and said, O altar, altar, thus saith the LORD; Behold, a child shall be born unto the house of David, Josiah by name; and upon thee shall he offer the priests of the high places that burn incense upon thee, and men's bones

shall be burnt upon thee.

³ And he gave a sign the same day, saying, This is the sign which the LORD hath spoken; Behold, the altar shall be rent, and the ashes that are upon it shall be poured out.

⁴ And it came to pass, when king Jeroboam heard the saying of the man of God, which had cried against the altar in Bethel, that he put forth his hand from the altar, saying, Lay hold on him. And his hand, which he put forth against him, dried up, so that he could not pull it in again to him.

⁵ The altar also was rent, and the ashes poured out from the altar, according to the sign which the man of God had given by the word of the LORD.

What an awesome way to be used by the Lord. I'm talking about a true prophet of the Lord that heard from God and acted on the call to the letter….at least in the beginning. However after this great move of God Jeroboam offered to feed him in his palace but the prophet refused due to the fact that God had told him to, well read it for yourself:

⁸ And the man of God said unto the king, If thou wilt give me half thine house, I will not go in with thee, neither will I eat bread nor drink water in this place:

⁹ For so was it charged me by the word of the LORD, saying, Eat no bread, nor drink water, nor turn again by the same way that thou camest.

¹⁰ So he went another way, and returned not by the way that he came to Bethel.

Ahh such an awe inspiring speech and initial action by the man of God right? But the story doesn't end there. And I'm here to let someone know that the glory is not contained in your fancy speech or what is done when everyone else is around, it's contained in the obedience of the details that God says are important after that. I don't care how loud you holler into that mic on Sunday or any other day it doesn't impress God and therefore doesn't impress me. The details of the matter are important and the only thing that should matter to you is what matters to God. If God is not getting any glory out of the deal you're treading on dangerous ground. Be careful not to get too impressed with yourself. Let's continue.

Later on in the chapter another "older" prophet heard what had happened in Bethel and commanded his donkey be saddled so that he could catch this "younger" prophet. He went to the young man and told him to come back with him to eat and drink. The young man told him the same instructions that God had given him that he told Jeroboam. However this older prophet told him **18** *He said unto him, I am a prophet also as thou art; and an angel spake unto me by the word of the LORD, saying, Bring him back with thee into thine house, that he may eat bread and drink water. But he lied unto him.*

To make a short story shorter the young man believed the lie because the older guy claimed to be a man of God that had heard something different from the Lord. He went back and ate and had a good time and you would never guess what happened.

[20] And it came to pass, as they sat at the table that the word of the LORD came unto the prophet that brought him back:
[21] And he cried unto the man of God that came from Judah, saying, Thus saith the LORD, Forasmuch as thou hast disobeyed the mouth of the LORD, and hast not kept the commandment which the LORD thy God commanded thee,
[22] But camest back, and hast eaten bread and drunk water in the place, of the which the Lord did say to thee, Eat no bread, and drink no water; thy carcase shall not come unto the sepulchre of thy fathers.
[23] And it came to pass, after he had eaten bread, and after he had drunk, that he saddled for him the ass, to wit, for the prophet whom he had brought back.
[24] And when he was gone, a lion met him by the way, and slew him: and his carcase was cast in the way, and the ass stood by it, the lion also stood by the carcase.
[25] And, behold, men passed by, and saw the carcase cast in the way, and the lion standing by the carcase: and they came and told it in the

city where the old prophet dwelt.

Such a shame but unfortunately this story is more common than you might think. One of the biggest ploys' that satan use against the body of Christ is distraction. And just like this story he'll use people that you respect and revere to do it if they allow him too. Not every body that says they're hearing from God really is. That's why you shouldn't just let anybody lay their hands on you and speak into your life. If you say Amen to everything that is spoken into your life you are consenting in the spirit world and giving license to the spirit behind the action of the person. Test the spirit by the spirit beloved. But how can you do that if you are not in the spirit yourself? The answer is you can't. So I would suggest that you learn the voice of God and how to feel His presence in yourself, in your situations, and in other people. When you master this you'll be a prime candidate that can endure to the end. Achieving this ability will make you a leader instead of a follower because hearing God's voice is the number one thing that the body of Christ is becoming unable to do.

Our ability to discern God from something else has been diluted and weakened which is why we're allowing everything under the sun to occur in the land. We're following the political correctness of the world and compromising our Christian values. Sure world take down the Ten Commandments, take prayer out of the schools, pass same sex laws, and advance your homosexual agenda. This is what we're saying by not standing on the wall for God even when He's telling us to yell from the rooftops that He's not pleased. Beloved, even when you're serving be a leader because being a follower can get you killed.

The final phase is the Expectation phase. You can't expect what is not yours. However God promised us that if His people who are called by His name would humble themselves, seek His face, get on their knees and pray, and turn from their wicked ways that He would hear our prayers from Heaven and He would answer them and heal our land. Refer to 2 Chronicles 7:14. You can't earn your salvation it's given only by His grace however there are certain levels of the blessed and victorious life that follows the initial salvation experience that you can expect from how well you can back up what you profess. God will give you plenty of opportunities to prove what you say concerning Him. If you say you love Him you show that by being obedient to His commands. Jesus said in John 14:15 ~ If you love me obey my commandments. In verse 21 he broke it down for us. **21** Whoever has my commands and obeys them, he is the one who loves me. He who loves me will be loved by my Father, and I too will love him and show myself to him."

Isn't it wonderful to know that all we have to do is keep our word and live a life that is acceptable to one person and that is God Himself for us to have the victorious life? God has given us the answers to every test. I'll leave you regarding the subject of this chapter with Ephesians 4:17-24

17) This I say therefore, and testify in the Lord, that ye henceforth walk not as other Gentiles walk, in the vanity of their mind, **18**) Having the understanding darkened, being alienated from the life of God through the ignorance that is in them, because of the blindness of their heart: **19**) Who being past feeling have given themselves over unto lasciviousness, to work all uncleanness with greediness. **20**) But ye have not so learned Christ; **21**) If so be that ye have heard him, and have been taught by him, as the truth is in Jesus: **22**) That ye put off concerning the former conversation the old man, which is corrupt according to the deceitful lusts; **23**) And be renewed in the spirit of your mind; **24**) And that ye put on the new man, which after God is created in righteousness and true holiness.

CHAPTER 6

Godly Leadership

We have to be secure in who we are to effectively lead someone else. The question, disagreement, and sometimes even criticism of another are "necessary" to engage in the process of growth. Teachers, don't abuse your students. Leaders, don't abuse your followers because you're only a steward for the real Master, for a season. Do exactly what He says and then get out of the way. As soon as we try to get cute, God gets ugly. Stay humble and let God fight your battles.

If we're doing exactly what God has told us to do the results is not on us, the results are on God. You see Moses ran into this trap in *Numbers 20* when God told him to speak to the rock to produce water for the Israelites that were in need. Thirty-Nine years later he had hit the rock and water was produced, however this time God had instructed him to "speak" to the rock. And a lot of times we're expecting God to answer our problems or issues the way that He did before or even the way that we've seen Him work in someone else life. But we have to understand that God never does anything the same way twice. Even if it's the littlest variance, He always moves in a different way. There are no two snowflakes that are the same. Every hair on our head is different from another. It has been scientifically proven that every piece of sand that has ever been created is different than another. Every cloud is different than another, every star, every planet and every person. This is all part of God's plan, it's all a part of the process.

This fact is sometimes a stumbling block to the believer and it shouldn't be. The longer that we live we should understand that things take time. And the things that are worth having and that we would want the most often take a little more time. You can't just throw a Thanksgiving Turkey in the microwave and cook it for Thanksgiving dinner. You have to clean it, gut it, season it, and baste it with butter or whatever oils you would use. Stuff it with stuffing and on and on until it's finally ready to be put into an oven where you will cook it at a certain temperature for many hours until its ready. During this time you will keep going back to observe this turkey which would include sometimes even opening the oven to ensure the meat of the turkey is being cooked correctly until it eventually becomes edible for consumption. Sometimes my mother and father because both of them were very good cooks would even stick a fork in the turkey to see how tender the meat was and to see the juice burst through the beautiful brown skin of the turkey onto the fork down the side of the turkey. And when the turkey finally passed this test is when the turkey was ready to be served to someone else.

God's way of doing things is higher than ours. Isaiah 55:8, 9 (TNIV) "For my thoughts are not your thoughts, neither are your ways my ways," declares the LORD. "As the heavens are higher than the earth, so are my ways higher than your ways and my thoughts than your thoughts." **God's process is always better than whatever our process would be.** I feel sorry for the person who never grows into this understanding. I feel sorry because this person will always be in a state of frustration wondering why things never work out according to their limited thought or mindset.

The fact that in Numbers 20, Moses hit the rock wasn't the problem. The hitting of the rock was only the symptom of the problem. The root of the problem is that Moses should've been able to at that point of his life to obey the simple instruction of the Lord regarding simply speaking to the rock. After all of the miracles that God performed through Moses, he of all people should've been able to exhibit the faith that it required to simply speak to his situation and watch it change. This passage of scripture in the Jewish world is called the Chukat. The translation of the Hebrew of this word means to "decree." It is the ninth word, and the first distinctive word, in the Weekly Torah Portion which is also known as Parshah. A Parshah is a section of the Torah (Hebrew Bible) that is read in Jewish services. It is the 39th weekly Torah portion (*parshah*) in the annual Jewish cycle of Torah reading and the sixth in the book of Numbers. It constitutes Numbers 19:1–22:1. Jews in the Diaspora generally read it in late June or July. In Judaism, the Torah is read publicly over the course of a year, with one major portion read each week in the Shabbat morning service.

The underlying meaning of what I'm explaining is that Moses

should've been able to declare and decree to the rock that water *will* flow forth. The fact that he instead hit the rock not only once but twice mind you and this showed God that if Moses couldn't get this basic principle, neither would anyone else during that particular time.

God had utilized Moses to deliver the Hebrews through miracle after miracle to declare plagues on a nation to the parting of the Red Sea. Moses should have matured to a point where he could've been used to simply speak to the issue or issues in his life and then trust God to address it. When we are in our spiritual infancy God will allow us to act out somewhat and address our situation. However, as we mature in our relationship with God He expects our faith to become mature as well. God intended to teach the Hebrew/Israelite people that the time of open miracles in the manner that they had seen were now over and that they were expected to live according to the power that was in them based off of their relationship with Him. Not that His power wasn't still there to deliver them in those miraculous ways but God was weaning them from having to rely on divine intervention at every stage of their walk with God.

God wasn't going to give them manna from Heaven anymore. He had determined that the quail would stop and that the pillars of fire that guided them by night and the clouds that guided them by day were now to be removed. He had literally led them by the hand in their infancy to show them who He was and demonstrate His commitment and power regarding their purpose and yet He expected them to get to the point where this was unnecessary.

God won't use what we don't choose. God wants us to willingly place our faith in Him. He won't ever force the issue. He won't ever make you do what you're supposed to do. He won't ever make you do what you don't want to. He'd rather be disappointed than to **force** you to put all of your trust in Him. The Bible says that without faith it's impossible to please God and so then we understand that our exhibited and innate faith is what attracts a Holy God to a guilty sinner.

Even though God told Moses to speak or "decree" to the rocks in front of the people, he hit it with his anointed staff twice. Not only did he use a different method than God desired, he ridiculed God's people, he called them rebels. Consider these verses:

Numbers Chapter 20 (NIV)

10. He and Aaron gathered the assembly together in front of the rock and Moses said to them, "Listen, you rebels, must we bring you water out of this rock?"

11. Then Moses raised his arm and struck the rock twice with his staff. Water gushed out, and the community and their livestock drank.

12. But the LORD said to Moses and Aaron, "Because you did not trust in me enough to honor me as holy in the sight of the Israelites, you will not bring this community into the land I give them."

God still moved in the case of Moses for the sake of the people and Moses' office but the consequence was the latter glory that Moses would've enjoyed if he didn't allow the people to get him frustrated. If I can impress anything to the spiritual leader that may be reading this book it would be this. **Do not become too impressed with yourself!** Don't make the same mistake that Moses made and talk about yourself and what **you're** doing or have done for those people that are assigned to your anointing. You haven't done anything that God hasn't given you the grace to do or equipped you for so don't lord your "accomplishments" over people.

To the senior deacon, evangelist, elder, pastor, bishop, apostle, prelate, prophet/prophetess and any other title for leader of God's people; God will honor certain things simply because of your office it doesn't mean that he's pleased with your decisions or your methods. Be careful that your attitude and emotions don't have you serving on borrowed time. Meaning that God could have a situation or someone prepared to remove you because of your rebellion. Remember your oath to the Lord to "serve" His people and be a good steward over His mysteries as it says in 1 Corinthians 4:1.

Moses was supposed to **speak** to the atmosphere and watch his situation change. God didn't want him to get any glory other than to be the visual demonstration and teacher as to what God expected. God was trying to teach His people that all you had to do was speak and He would hear them. I'm sure that God was saying to Himself after Moses' failure that if you want something done right you got to do it yourself. And of course I'm poking a little fun at this story. The moral: Don't take credit for God's work.

CHAPTER 7

The Law of the Spirit of Life/ The Law of Sin and Death

The Law of the Spirit of Life has set us free from the Law of Sin and Death. The epic battle between these two laws takes us back to creation and even before it. The privilege that we have today regarding our ability to know certain ancient truths that were once mysteries and in part still is, required someone to gain access into God's Glory.

I want to impart into your Spirit reader that unless you have the courage and take the necessary steps of preparation and positioning that it requires to ENTER INTO God's Glory....you will never find your ultimate purpose. ***You won't ever enter into God's Glory, His Holy of Holies, and the inner most chambers of His Spirit unless you have Relationship.***

Moses' disobedience was a symbol of a deeper problem that

God couldn't accept at this point of his development and it derailed Moses entrance into the Promised Land and also subsequently caused God to shorten his life. For the wages of sin is death.

His hitting the rock for the second time was a problem because the rock was a symbol of something so much deeper In order to do this topic justice let's go to the New Testament. I would be doing a great dishonor however, if I don't explain the major theme of the 8th Chapter of Romans before going forward. The theme of this Romans 8 revolves around two extremes or two Ancient Laws. One as we see in verse 2 is the Law of the Spirit of Life and the other is the Law of Sin and Death.

Romans 8 (NIV)
Rom 8:2 for the law of the Spirit of life in Christ Jesus has made me free from the law of sin and death.
Rom 8:3 For what the law could not do in that it was weak through the flesh, God did by sending His own Son in the likeness of sinful flesh, on account of sin: He condemned sin in the flesh,
Rom 8:4 that the righteous requirement of the law might be fulfilled in us who do not walk according to the flesh but according to the Spirit.

The Holy Spirit empowers us to live according to "the law of the Spirit of life in Christ Jesus." And, if we walk in the power of the Spirit, we fulfill the requirements of the law.

Romans 8 (NIV)

Verses 13-18 talk about Life through the Spirit

13 For if you live according to the sinful nature, you will die; but if by the Spirit you put to death the misdeeds of the body, you will live, **14** because those who are led by the Spirit of God are sons of God. **15** For you did not receive a spirit that makes you a slave again to fear, but you received the Spirit of sonship. And by him we cry, ""Abba," Father." **16** The Spirit himself testifies with our spirit that we are God's children. **17** Now if we are children, then we are heirs--heirs of God and co-heirs with Christ, if indeed we share in his sufferings in order that we may also share in his glory.

Verses 13-27 refer to our Future Glory
18 I consider that our present sufferings are not worth comparing with the glory that will be revealed in us. **19** The creation waits in eager expectation for the sons of God to be revealed. **20** For the creation was subjected to frustration, not by its own choice, but by the will of the one who subjected it, in hope **21** that the creation itself will be liberated from its bondage to decay and brought into the glorious freedom of the children of God. **22** We know that the whole creation has been groaning as in the pains of childbirth right up to the present time. **23** Not only so, but we ourselves, who have the first fruits of the Spirit, groan inwardly as we wait eagerly for our adoption as sons, the redemption of our bodies. **24** For in this hope we were saved. But hope that is seen is no hope at all. Who hopes for what he already has? **25** But if we hope for what we do not yet have, we wait for it patiently. **26** In the same way, the Spirit helps us in our weakness. We do not know what we ought to pray for, but the Spirit himself intercedes for us with groans that words cannot express. **27** And he who searches our hearts knows the mind of the Spirit, because the Spirit intercedes for the saints in accordance with God's will.

Verses 28-31 declares that we are More than Conquerors
28 And we know that in all things God works for the good of those who love him, who have been called according to his purpose. **29** For those God foreknew he also predestined to be conformed to the likeness of his Son, that he might be the firstborn among many brothers. **30** And those he predestined, he also called; those he called, he also justified; those he justified, he also glorified. **31** What, then, shall we say in response to this? If God is for us, who can be against us?

Everything that we know about creation and even what happened before it as a Christian is because God allowed someone special access into His Glory to retrieve the information for dissemination to the rest of us. This person as we know it initially was Moses.
If it wasn't for Moses being considered worthy of God for whatever reason we would not know the real way in which the world was cre-

ated for example. Or the real way that man was created or even woman for that matter. God took me to Adam as I reflected on this fact.

Do you know that Adam was the only truly "created" human being ever? He was formed from the dust of the earth by the very hands of God. He was breathed on by the very mouth of the Creator! And lo and behold he was.

I like to say that Adam fell from Relationship to Revelation in the process of falling from God's grace by following Eve and ultimately disobeying God's commandment. You're asking yourself how he fell from relationship to revelation. Let me tell you how this occurred. When Adam was formed he literally walked the garden with God. He had a relationship with Him as is evident in him knowing his duties of naming everything that was on the ground, in the ground, in the waters, and over the fowl of the air. He knew that he had dominion over every creeping thing etc. He didn't get his instructions from a Bible he got understood his duties because God communicated with him directly.

The next few things I'm going to surmise about Adam might rub some of you the wrong way however let me expand your thinking. Adam wasn't quite like you and I. The Garden of Eden is said to be about 3000 to 5000 miles in diameter. We can approximate this by looking at the rivers that encompassed it, such as the Euphrates and Tigris. It is humanly impossible for any mere man to ever walk 3000 to 5000 miles at any one time over a set amount of time. So how did Adam fulfill his duty of naming everything on the Earth? Are you ready for this? He probably thought his way to where he wanted to go.

And then on top of that since he had to take care of everything that was in the sea he probably just walked on the water in the same manner that Jesus did. Because he didn't know that he wasn't supposed to do this. And then to blow your mind even further as I'm smiling, Adam probably flew because he had to be able to identify the birds or fowls of the air and what better way to do it then to meet them in the air.

If we substitute the word disorder for sin we understand that the wages of disorder which is the opposite of process is separation and death. Sin is the rejection of God's rightful authority in our lives. So for the normal layperson it is important to not reject God's guidance and commandments concerning how we are to live and move and have our being. For the spiritual leader it is doubly important whereas you are held to a higher standard due to a greater responsibility that God has emplaced on and entrusted to you.

Consider others to be higher than yourselves and lead in holy reverence to the God who has ordained you. Live the Word, teach the Word, preach the Word, feed the hungry, minister to the sick, make disciples and then get out of the way. The biggest problem for some of our spiritual leaders is the same one that Moses had; they don't know how to get out of the way. The ultimate barometer of how effective a leader is or was is in the duplication of himself or herself in their organization. It is said that imitation is the ultimate flattery. If you are a pastor of a church and no one in that organization wants to be like you or become a pastor you're doing something wrong. If no one wants to flow under the same anointing that you do you might be in the wrong place. Maybe you should be on staff instead of being the leader because **effective leadership has to affect.**

Larry Edward Birchett, Jr.

CHAPTER 8

*S*piritual *A*uthority and *L*eadership

The fire that ignites other fires shine best and will never be diminished.

Pastor Larry Edward Birchett, Jr.

I stated in my previous book, Reverence for the Storm, that I believe the Church Age as we know it will soon come to an end. I don't believe in mega churches and minor ministry. If the pastor is the only one in the church with the Mercedes Benz or Rolls Royce that's not God. If the pastor is the only one with the big house, this is not God's intention. This is why as the leader you should be pushing and praying for the prosperity of your people as much as you can. Let's go deeper. If the pastor is the only ministry going on in the church, this is not God. There is a saying out there that says if you put a *"little man"* in a big church it will only be a matter of time before that *"little man"* brings that church down to his level. This is why self esteem and being secure in who **you** are is mandatory for the successful leader. And please don't confuse what I'm referring to with false humility because that is one of the poor leader mantles as well. God never intended for any one person to be the only voice that He speaks to His people through for the rest of their life to the point that a person feels stifled and stagnant. Even if you were able to eat Filet Mignon every night you would hate it after a month. No one person has a word from the Lord all of the time. God is a God of fresh oil and as leaders we have to know where that fresh oil is supposed to come from. The fresh oil can come from anybody on any given day.

I, being a young pastor, believe that the pastor should be the prevailing voice in the house of God however; I'm a proponent of variety and the manifest presence of God being allowed to operate in the building. I can remember the days when the pastor would get up to preach and God would let him know that the service wasn't on him today. He would call a certain deacon, a mother of the church, minister, elder, or maybe even associate pastor up to give the word because God had instructed him to do so. I've seen two great men, Apostle Earl Palmer and Bishop Raymond Baylor do this more than once and the service would always be awesome. Why? Because the man or woman of God was obedient to the voice of the Lord, secure in his or her position, and free to exercise the liberty of God's many gifts in the house. 1 Corinthians 12:14(KJV) says; *For the body is not one member, but many.* Sometimes God may want to do surgery in His people through the musicians and His music, sometimes He might want to work through His children. He might want to use the testimony of the lady in the back row to bless the whole church and be the only Word that the people are to hear for that day. Are you listening for the voice of the Lord men and women of God? Or are you trying to figure out how to create the best performance week after week after week.

I, having served as a Captain in the US Army as everything from Platoon Leader, Maintenance Control Officer, Executive Officer, Battalion S4, Brigade S4, Battalion S1/ Adjutant and a host of other titles and duties have always believed in what I call "spreading the wealth." From having come from the ranks of the enlisted up to the commissioned officer I know what it's like to follow good and bad leaders and I remember the good times and the bad. I remember the good leaders and the bad ones that thought they were the best. The overriding trait of the good leader is the ability to control their power and authority which I wrap up in one word; humility, and they will always get others involved in the process of their leadership.

The trained leader knows and understands that there has to be an effective structure in place supported by a firm foundation. This structure goes in the form of a curved end triangle for me not a pointy one because the pointy model doesn't leave room for flexibility and any exception that God may have placed in your particular organization. What is true of the basic shape of the triangle is that there is always less "sanctioned" leaders than those that are being led even though everyone should be empowered to understand that everyone is a leader. I know that went over some of your heads but keep following me and the Holy Spirit will soon bring illumination to you. The fatty part of the triangle is the foundation that will cause the structure/organization to stand. If the organization was built right, the leader can be taken out of the picture and the organization will still stand and function on its own until a new leader is selected. That's why the equation can't be the other way around, if everyone is a leader then as people transcend into different parts of their lives maybe at no fault of their own or the leader, as soon as they leave or are removed the structure will start to crumble. Or there will be a conflict until the gaping hole is repaired.

Our churches can't be built on personality. We understand however, that everyone has a preference. **Don't allow preference to become your only reference**. **Don't allow your experience to become your only convictions.** I like to teach that the Word of God doesn't need our help we're just supposed to declare it and let it do it's work. Once it is declared, taught, and preached with authority and understanding it is the Holy Spirit's job to perform the work. Isaiah 55:11(KJV) says; *So shall my word be that goeth forth out of my mouth: it shall not return unto me void, but it shall accomplish that which I please, and it shall prosper in the thing whereto I sent it.* If the Word doesn't say it don't you say it! I beat this point up in my prior book so I won't go there again nevertheless don't say God has declared sin on something that is merely your conviction. This will absolutely destroy the validity of the Gospel. This goes from your view on wine to the internet to Gospel Rap to taking medicine or what goes on in the marriage bed. All of these things only create unnecessary bondage to a man's law. Whereas God's law does not label any of the aforementioned things, in themselves sin. Refer to Galatians 3 and let's move on.

Spread the wealth men and women of God and watch God's ministry grow. You notice I didn't say your ministry because that's where the problem lies with the average spiritual leader. As soon as you realize that all of this Kingdom work that you're doing is really not about you, the sooner God can take the lid off of your potential and utilize everybody in your church or organization to their fullest and I mean fullest capability.

My wife, Joanna, is an awesome minister of the Gospel of Christ. She has operated under the grace of her call as an Evangelist and is now serving as the Co-Pastor of the beloved ministry that God has entrusted to our stewardship, Harvest House Restoration Center. She is used mightily by God via the TV talk show called Gospel 4 U Ministry TV Talk Show, a Christian publication called Gospel 4 U Magazine, she's often called on to praise dance, she goes out to preach, and on and on and on. And a lot of people marvel at the fact that I "allow" this, have no issues with it, not threatened by her, and am her biggest encourager. I look at them and always ask why? I always say this is not about me or her. This is about the calling on both of our lives. If I as being the priest of my home and her earthly covering do not allow her to express herself in the way that God has designed her then I will be severely hurting her even to the point of abuse and sinning against her because I'd be keeping God's purpose from being realized in and through her. So many men do that to their anointed wives. And what results normally is a life of waste on behalf of the woman because of the small minded and insecure man.

Her being used doesn't change the fact that I'm her husband. It doesn't change the fact that the husband is the head of the wife and is to love the wife as Christ loved the church. It doesn't change the fact that I am the physical and spiritual leader in our house and joint ministry. All it means is that she has many gifts that she's not afraid to use for the Kingdom. It means that I'm secure enough to allow someone else to operate at the same level and anointing and even higher if God says so for His purpose and His glory. And that is what God is looking for in His leaders. The fact that so many people are blessed by her life is a testament to her being under good covering that is not afraid of her development and growth. David was this kind of leader and this is one of the reasons why God called him a man after His own heart. Always remember this, a leader that purposely diminishes the leadership gifts of another is an insecure leader.

I believe that if you don't honor the anointing of another person you shouldn't expect anyone to honor yours. At the same time this model has to go both ways. God loved David because he wasn't ashamed of his relationship with God and exemplified Godly leadership. David served with many men that were fiercer than he. They loved him and honored him because they knew he was fair and they could flow in their gifting as well. In II Samuel 23 we will notice that it is the end of David's life and reign as King and it is as if he is reflecting back over his life. He reflects back over his life and the great men that God had sent his way:

II Samuel 23 (TNIV)

[8] These are the names of David's mighty warriors:
Josheb-Basshebeth, a Tahkemonite, was chief of the Three; he raised his spear against eight hundred men, whom he killed in one encounter.
[9] Next to him was Eleazar son of Dodai the Ahohite. As one of the three mighty warriors, he was with David when they taunted the Philistines gathered at Pas Dammim for battle. Then the Israelites retreated, [10] but Eleazar stood his ground and struck down the Philistines till his hand grew tired and froze to the sword. The LORD brought about a great victory that day. The troops returned to Eleazar, but only to strip

the dead.

¹¹ Next to him was Shammah son of Agee the Hararite. When the Philistines banded together at a place where there was a field full of lentils, Israel's troops fled from them. ¹² But Shammah took his stand in the middle of the field. He defended it and struck the Philistines down, and the LORD brought about a great victory.

¹³ During harvest time, three of the thirty chief warriors came down to David at the cave of Adullam, while a band of Philistines was encamped in the Valley of Rephaim. ¹⁴ At that time David was in the stronghold, and the Philistine garrison was at Bethlehem. ¹⁵ David longed for water and said, "Oh, that someone would get me a drink of water from the well near the gate of Bethlehem!" ¹⁶ So the three mighty warriors broke through the Philistine lines, drew water from the well near the gate of Bethlehem and carried it back to David. But he refused to drink it; instead, he poured it out before the LORD. ¹⁷ "Far be it from me, LORD, to do this!" he said. "Is it not the blood of men who went at the risk of their lives?" And David would not drink it.

Such were the exploits of the three mighty warriors.

¹⁸ Abishai the brother of Joab son of Zeruiah was chief of the Three. He raised his spear against three hundred men, whom he killed, and so he became as famous as the Three. ¹⁹ Was he not held in greater honor than the Three? He became their commander, even though he was not included among them.

²⁰ Benaiah son of Jehoiada, a valiant fighter from Kabzeel, performed great exploits. He struck down Moab's two mightiest warriors. He also went down into a pit on a snowy day and killed a lion. ²¹ And he struck down a huge Egyptian. Although the Egyptian had a spear in his hand, Benaiah went against him with a club. He snatched the spear from the Egyptian's hand and killed him with his own spear. ²² Such were the exploits of Benaiah son of Jehoiada; he too was as famous as the three mighty warriors. ²³ He was held in greater honor than any of the Thirty, but he was not included among the Three. And David put him in charge of his bodyguard.

In short, David served with men who could probably out "Soldier" him and it didn't stop him from exhibiting strong and successful leadership over them. In verse 15 David "longed" for some water when they were surrounded by the Philistines and three of his mighty warriors broke through the camp, risking their very lives just to bring this man a glass of water. Oh what a testament to a leader that was loved and honored so much that they would risk their lives. Would anyone risk their life just for your comfort? Honor and respect the diversity of others and they will honor you men and women of God. Don't be afraid to say publicly that this person is awesome in this or that. It may even require for you to say that a person is better than you at something and its okay. The people that God has assigned to you will appreciate you for the honesty and your ability to ensure that they are not deficient in anything. Keep them encouraged and feed from the inside first. ***Seek their hearts and not their hands.***

Don't esteem and promote others from outside of the organization more than you do your own. This is just like talking about your neighbors kids more than you do your own. And please don't flaunt your prejudices and biases in front of them. Because even your kids will rise up and rebel openly against you if you continue with this error filled behavior. All of these things are not the fault of the organization it is the fault of the leader because the leader sowed prejudice and discord.

If you don't display prejudice and are secure in your mantle of leadership you will be free to promote at will. You never should make excuses for a promotion when it is warranted. Everything and everybody in life is in a process of development and you do not want to be the person that hinders that development. If you're not prepared to duplicate yourself in the ministry then you will become the tyrant or maybe a better word is warden that everyone that is ready to operate at a higher level despises because you're standing in their way. So **don't make your process longer than God's process.** Also never impose your experience on everyone else after you especially if you know that your experience is way out of the norm. It would have been foolish for Moses to say to Joshua that unless God speaks to him from a burning bush like God had did him he wasn't really called to be a leader. God never does the same thing twice and is not silly, so don't you be!

No one stays in school there entire life in any area of study even though the truth is that we're always constantly learning. Church education and spiritual development is no different. Put an end date on your curriculum and let God continue the rest of the training. Don't make life indentured contracts with people that God have chosen *you* to "disciple." When it is clear that someone should be placed in training for a Deacon, Evangelist, Minister, Elder, Prophet/Prophetess or Pastor make sure that they are placed in that training program for a set amount of time. I'm tailoring my comments specifically on leadership to the church because we as church leaders have a tendency to be so deep that it's hard for someone to tell us the truth. Meanwhile the world is looking at our process and shaking their head because they think we're a bunch of emotional power hungry amateurs in places of influence over weak-minded and lowly people, which is not the case at all. Leadership is a learned ability in every walk of life. I don't care who you are you can learn too.

If you don't take the time to establish discipleship curriculum at least take the time to establish the duration of active discipleship. If God has not spoken to you concerning the person that you're disciple*ing* don't disciple them for leadership just allow them to continue to grow and serve God with all of the fervor that they've always had. It's nothing wrong with that beloved. God is not a respecter of titles; He is not a respecter of persons.

In his book, Emotional Intelligence, psychologist Dr. Daniel Goleman says that IQ amounts to only 20 percent of success. To keep your job and earn a promotion, you need more than intelligence. The difference between the corner church and the thriving church a lot of times is contained in their organizational leadership and ethics or there lack thereof. When you are part of a well ran organization you will never be frustrated because of the lack of opportunity and procedure. Procedures and regulations will be well stated and understood whereas no offense can occur. This requires preparation on behalf of the leader.

Frustration only hinders the work of the ministry and should be avoided at all costs. The small church mentality will be that processes are unnecessary and that everything is decided by a lightning flash in the mind of the senior leader or a "word from the Lord." This is simply incorrect and is producing a generation of "I've got something to prove" pastor/leaders that are operating with strange spirits. And before we judge these leaders we have to look at the individuals who "developed" them. If this chapter is tough to take for you pastor, or you elder, or bishop, or apostle, it's meant to challenge you. Time is winding down and I long for the time when the church operates on one accord in excellence. No other organization should outclass us in regards to how we handle our affairs because God Himself has set up His priest hood from even before the Levitical Order and onward.

Leaders add value to those that would follow, imposters and imitators take value. Preaching ability doesn't make you the pastor dear one. Ensure that God has deposited within you the gift of leadership and that you have a shepherds heart. If you know you're lacking these traits and believe that God is calling you to one day take the mantle of one of His fellowships ensure that you get the training necessary to fulfill every expectation that God has for you and lead with integrity. Establish a reasonable time of preparation and stick to the agreement, because the relationship of student/teacher is definitely an agreement worthy of contractual obligations. No one likes to waste their time doing anything. The church should be the last institution that would want to waste anyone's time.

Don't let your experience drive your convictions. Just because you became a Deacon at the age of 55 doesn't mean that everyone in the world has to follow this model. Just because you were the janitor and somehow was selected for Pastor doesn't mean that this is God's model for promotion. Get over your past and review each case individually. Be strong enough to say that this person is called and should be set on this course because this call has been made known to you by God Himself and there are no excuses to be given in its regards. Sometimes this will require you to send some of your leaders out because God will tell you that He has a work for them that do not require them to necessarily walk side by side with you.

Some of you are saying I'm not trying to hear this right now and who is this young guy to give me advice anyway? I got news for you this is for you and God has sent me directly to you! You're the one who probably needs to read this three and four times before you go and meet with your leaders and keep all of this in the back of your mind while you're at it. I pray that God gives you the humility to receive true instruction from the Lord and the conviction of heart to do it the way that God wants it done. **Remember that whenever God gives a Word it goes through the vessel that delivers the message first so all of this applies to me as well.**

In the end there can only be one leader and this is God's biblical model. Leaders, part of the process of training someone else for ministry is to watch and access the spirit of the disciple while they're *in* process. A successful candidate will remain humble and will always stay in character if they truly have the servant spirit necessary to serve God's people. *1 Peter 5:6 says Therefore humble yourselves under the mighty hand of God, that He may exalt you in due time*

As they're going through the process ensure that this conversation is had and their assessment in this area is a part of your quarterly counseling. Which means that yes you should be conducting quarterly sessions with your ministerial staff not as a threatening tool but as a time of direction and encouragement. Communication eliminates confusion.

Communicate clearly your vision for the ministry and for them. They will either respect your clarity or have an allergic reaction to it. They have to respect the anointing of somebody else, namely you, before they're put into a position of leadership and mentorship. Elijah told Elisha that if he was there with him when he was taken up into Heaven, God would give him a double portion of the anointing. He didn't mince words, he was clear and direct. It was up to Elisha to accept the challenge or reject it. Consider the text:

2 Kings 2:9-11 ^{9}And it came to pass, when they were gone over, that Elijah said unto Elisha, Ask what I shall do for thee, before I be taken away from thee. And Elisha said, I pray thee, let a double portion of thy spirit be upon me.

¹⁰And he said, Thou hast asked a hard thing: nevertheless, if thou see me when I am taken from thee, it shall be so unto thee; but if not, it shall not be so.
¹¹And it came to pass, as they still went on, and talked, that, behold, there appeared a chariot of fire, and horses of fire, and parted them both asunder; and Elijah went up by a whirlwind into heaven.
¹²And Elisha saw it, and he cried, My father, my father, the chariot of Israel, and the horsemen thereof. And he saw him no more: and he took hold of his own clothes, and rent them in two pieces.
¹³He took up also the mantle of Elijah that fell from him, and went back, and stood by the bank of Jordan;
¹⁴And he took the mantle of Elijah that fell from him, and smote the waters, and said, Where is the LORD God of Elijah? and when he also had smitten the waters, they parted hither and thither: and Elisha went over.
¹⁵And when the sons of the prophets which were to view at Jericho saw him, they said, The spirit of Elijah doth rest on Elisha. And they came to meet him, and bowed themselves to the ground before him.

Elisha got the message, accepted the challenge, and prevailed thereby receiving the benefits of sonship from Elijah which is important and the event was the inauguration of his leadership role as he received Elijah's mantle and was two times as powerful as the man of God.

The assigning of individuals without them first learning the lesson of followership can be fatal for anyone that they have influence over and will result in more of a *tormentorship* than a mentorship. A great resource on that topic is 'The Cry of a Generation; When Torn Mentors become Tormentors' by my friend and awesome man of God, Pastor Lawrence Moore. Excellent book on the topic.

A lot of what I've already discussed is the normal duties of the Pastor, Bishop, Priest, or Apostle. The Bishop and the Apostle should have really duplicated these efforts many times in their oversight of many ministries and or building fellowships and churches. The overseeing of churches is the work of the Bishop and the Apostle is used in the same way however they're God sent to build fellowships and establish works. In our day and time we have pastors with barely 50 members calling themselves Bishops, let alone Apostle. God help us. However, this new practice comes from the lust of power, low self esteem, and the want of prestige as well as a prevailing ignorance that has crept in the halls of administration in our church governments.

Matthew 19:14 (NIV) says: Jesus said, "Let the little children come to me, and do not hinder them, for the kingdom of heaven belongs to such as these." If there are any of us that think we're the end all/ be all of everything that is spiritual normally that's the sign to indicate that we're probably not. And you'll sometimes see that those of "us" that carry this kind of attitude hinder others from being themselves, from growing, and from truly seeking after God. Piousness, pride, and even the proud look is an abhorrence to God therefore let us all remember the beautiful words of Jesus that says "Do to others as you would have them do to you." Luke 6:31 (NIV). Be blessed leaders of God's people and remember; the fear of the LORD teaches a man wisdom, and humility comes before honor. Proverbs 15:33 (NIV)

CHAPTER 9

Mirage

I believe one's speech is largely the result of his or her perspective. Generally, people's perspectives are born from the height in which they think. My question to you is, "How high are you speaking and thinking?" ~ TD Jakes

---

Don't chase mirages. Mirages are like illusions and the devil specializes in illusions. Illusions are satanic dreams. In other words lies. satan showed Eve and Adam a mirage that they regrettably believed and hence it caused them paradise. Lesson: don't allow anyone to make you leave your God ordained place of purpose for the mirage. Your unstableness will lead to your demise. Your inability to discern the authentic from the copy will be a very critical deficiency to overcome. God will lead you into an area of life and purpose that is most natural, the area you were created for. satan's job is to show you the mirage which will lead you away from this purpose. Your job is to tell him to "get thee behind" you.

On the morning of November 22, 2011, I was in the master bathroom getting ready for work when I heard my wife speaking in her sleep. I peeked around to look at her and she was squirming in the bed and saying "No! No! No!" and was crying as she seemed to be getting more irritated. I approached the bed and shook her on her arm and called out "Joanna! Joanna!" She woke up in a daze like with red eyes and tears coming down her face. I asked her what was wrong and she said she had a dream. Of course the inevitable question was what did you dream about? I finally asked her this and she proceeded to tell me.

She explained that a person in all white clothes appeared before her bed. She was startled of course and the individual told her to not be afraid, "I'm not here to harm you." She then found herself elevating off of the bed and was taken outside of the window where she bowed down because she said she was scared and somehow she knew not to look up. However whenever she would try to look up, the person would say "Don't look up!" Mind you our bedroom was on the second floor of a 2Plex home in New Jersey and therefore she realized that she was in the air. She said she looked around and saw me walking out of the front door of the house with an individual in white behind me as well. She said that I looked up at her with the kind of look as if to say what is she doing out here? Joanna, then said that the person, who she noticed had a sword like the one that she had seen in images of the great Ark Angel Michael, spoke and said "Tell Larry, these respectable sins; lust, anger, adultery, and arrogance."

I wrestled with this dream after my wife gave it to me because I had just finished a time of prayer that lasted about 21 days when this happened. During this time of prayer and fasting God had visited me in my dreams and hadn't given me any of these chastisements. God burst my bubble with the message because I had been asking Him to show me, me. I wanted to know anything that would cause me to miss Heaven or anything that would render me powerless against the kingdom of darkness and He hit me right between the eyes in a way that I had to listen and couldn't shrug it off. We sometime try to live in our own little worlds that we create for our selves thinking that we are insulated because of works. Because we have fasted for forty days and nights we believe that the world will change and that our flesh will no longer be an issue. God let me understand that this dream was sent to make me extremely focused. I was living in a mirage, a self made world that I created for myself that believed that because some things were socially acceptable that everything was okay and God said no.

Some sins have almost become respectable in this last generation but God is neither a respecter of persons nor a respecter of sin. We sometimes think that the big ones like murder, witchcraft, idolatry, and abortion are God's biggest pet peeves but God wants us to know that an illicit thought is just as offensive to Him and is considered adultery. He wants us to know that an argumentative spirit is not of God even when you're right and even though you say sorry afterwards you have an issue with anger; and thinking that you can operate in the deep things of God while operating in this manner is arrogance. It seems we've created a sliding scale where gossip, jealousy, and selfishness comfortably exist within the church. In short, some sins have simply become socially acceptable but God is saying to the church and He let me know specifically that He's calling me higher. He has a higher standard for us and that we can't operate like the world and claim that we're different. We are to be the light of the world. Just as the moon reflects the light of the sun we're supposed to reflect the light of the Son. The enemy will coax you into believing that you're okay however the Word of God says the following succinctly in ten verses:

1 Peter 1:15-25 King James Version (KJV)

[15] But as He which hath called you is holy, so be ye holy in all manner of conversation;

[16] Because it is written, Be ye holy; for I am holy.

[17] And if ye call on the Father, who without respect of persons judgeth according to every man's work, pass the time of your sojourning here in fear:

[18] Forasmuch as ye know that ye were not redeemed with corruptible things, as silver and gold, from your vain conversation received by tradition from your fathers;

[19] But with the precious blood of Christ, as of a lamb without blemish and without spot:

[20] Who verily was foreordained before the foundation of the world, but was manifest in these last times for you,

[21] Who by him do believe in God, that raised him up from the dead, and gave him glory; that your faith and hope might be in God.

[22] Seeing ye have purified your souls in obeying the truth through the Spirit unto unfeigned love of the brethren, see that ye love one another with a pure heart fervently:

[23] Being born again, not of corruptible seed, but of incorruptible, by the word of God, which liveth and abideth for ever.

²⁴ For all flesh is as grass, and all the glory of man as the flower of grass. The grass withereth, and the flower thereof falleth away:

²⁵ But the word of the Lord endureth for ever. And this is the word which by the gospel is preached unto you.

God is speaking into your life and you have to know God's voice for yourself. I'm relating this story because of verse 22 that tells us to purify our souls by obeying the truth through the Spirit and the fact that I love pleasing God more than pleasing myself and pleasing people. I write books because of the burden that God has placed inside of me to reach the world for Christ and assist in their spiritual growth.

Beloved please understand that even though before her dream I would have said that I wasn't any of those things, God wanted me to understand that He knew my heart and that's the most important part of us. God wanted me to understand that He is not just the judge of our physical nature He is the judge of our souls. We purify our souls by obeying the truth which is contained in the Holy Spirit, whom if we don't know, we can never claim to know the truth. I'm not a perfect person but I serve a God who is. All of the righteousness that I possess is that which God imputes to me through His son Jesus. After my 21 day prayer the pronouncement was not what I expected and not what I imagined the fruit of my relationship and progress with God would be at that point. And that is when God showed me Matthew 4 once again:

¹Then Jesus was led by the Spirit into the wilderness to be tempted by the devil. ² After fasting forty days and forty nights, he was hungry. ³ The tempter came to him and said, "If you are the Son of God, tell these stones to become bread."
⁴ Jesus answered, "It is written: 'Man shall not live on bread alone, but on every word that comes from the mouth of God.'

What was Jesus trying to say to me? He wanted me to see that it was right after He Himself had finished His forty day fast that His strength and resolve was tested. Beloved when the enemy see that you are acquiring power in the spiritual realm he will try to make you think that you don't have that power. In other words your greatest vulnerabilities will come after your greatest victories. satan will always bring up your past
because he has no control over your future. So whenever he or anyone brings railing accusations against you just understand that God is never in this type of behavior because God is not in the condemning business. God wasn't condemning me, He just wanted me to keep the spiritual gain that I've acquired and stay focused. As Psalms 30:5 states *His anger lasts but for a moment……..* Doesn't this make you glad?

In John 8, they brought a woman to Jesus right after He had finished teaching. She'd been caught in the very act of adultery and they wanted to get Jesus' permission to stone her as was the Jewish custom. They were trying to trip Jesus up and get Him in trouble with His followers. The next thing that Jesus did was so fascinating. *John 8:6~ They were using this question as a trap, in order to have a basis for accusing him. But Jesus bent down and started to write on the ground with his finger.*

You're asking yourself what is so special about this. Beloved have you ever considered the fact that Jesus never wrote a letter, a pamphlet, a booklet, let alone a book? Paul wrote letters which comprise of more than a half of the New Testament. Jesus was the very one that the whole Bible is written about and He never published one piece of work! Isn't this an amazing fact that leads to quite a few other questions? I believe that Jesus in His deity as being God in the flesh had to complete His mission without writing a single piece of work. He could only accomplish and fulfill His destiny by His spoken words, actions, and deeds. This is why Jesus was always careful with His words because He had creative power. He had the ability to create with His voice just as He did in Genesis when He said Let there be. I believe that whenever He wrote anything it created and/or changed things according to the creative power that was within Him. He came to fulfill the law and if He wrote something in regards to things it could've had a big impact on the world spiritually and possibly make things easier for Him which would've been illegal and classified as a transgression against the rules that He was supposed to live by. I believe He wrote something on the ground that changed the very destiny of the woman that was considered guilty. Jesus in His wisdom used the dirt of the ground because it would not be a permanent record of what He wrote and consequently the wind would blow His writing away. This is why some say that the written word is stronger than the spoken word; however one must understand that one must first hear the word to write it.

Consequently, whatever He wrote had to come to pass and the woman's life was spared and even written about in His holy book, His holy record, the Bible as a result of what He wrote into existence and His challenge to the condemners of the woman. He challenged them. He said he that is without sin, cast the first stone. What a challenge, what a lesson. Of course none of them were without sin and they all left from the oldest to the youngest. When He looked up he saw the woman standing there and asked her, 'Woman where are your condemners?' She acknowledged that they all had left. He said just as none of them had condemned her, neither did He. Who wouldn't serve a God like that?

God is like the sun, you can't look at it but without it you can't see everything else. So if your God is nice and neat and can be explained and understood you're probably looking at the moon or something else inferior because our God is an awesome wonder that cannot be fully explained or comprehended. He is the Alpha and Omega, the Beginning and the End, the Lily of the Valley from where everything has originated and will become.

CHAPTER 10

*P*erspective

I heard an awesome story one day from Dr. David Jeremiah, founder of Turning Point Radio and Television Ministries and senior pastor of Shadow Mountain Community Church when he visited the Giant Center for an awesome one day conference in Hershey, PA. The story is about a little girl that wandered onto a set of train tracks.

A locomotive was flying down the tracks as it had done day after day for months on a particular route. A person near the front of the train was looking out in front of the train and thought they saw a little girl way up yonder playing on the tracks. It was told to the conductor and the conductor didn't believe that little blip in the distance was a person. As the train got closer he readily acknowledged that it was in fact a little girl ahead on the tracks. The brakes were immediately applied to the train but because of the mass and the velocity of the train it didn't come to a complete stop. It did slow down however but not slow enough. The rate of speed was slowed to 40 mph then to 30 mph to 20 mph to 15 mph. Unfortunately not slow enough but a worker on the train hopped into action. He went out on the front of the train and leaned off of it anticipating the train's impact with the little girl. It was discovered that this man was a Vietnam Veteran and as the train slowed to 10 mph and came upon the little girl on the tracks he proceeded to kick her off of the tracks. He kicked her off of the tracks and she fell down the side of the mountain resulting in a chipped tooth and a broken arm.

If you were to only tune into this story at the very last minute, you would think that a very cruel thing has just happened to this little girl. You would probably say that the man that kicked the little girl should be locked up and is evil. But the truth of the matter is that he saved the little girl's life. His action allowed her to live another day. It allowed her to not have to go through the pain of being run over alive by a multi-ton train and suffering a horrible death. But if you didn't see what transpired before you wouldn't understand why she had to suffer a little discomfort in comparison to what she was about to suffer. If you didn't know what was about to happen to her should she hadn't been kicked by the man you might've cried and said how cruel! Or better yet how could God allow such a thing?

Sometimes the things that you think God has allowed to hurt you has been allowed to save you and your families life. Yeah you might have a few scrapes and scars but they're just reminders that God is a Restorer and Healer. And even now you don't look like what you've been through. So if I were you, I would give God praise right now no matter where you're at. If I were you I'd tell Him how thankful you are right now!

When I was going through some major challenges in my life, I remember complaining to God that this is unbearable. But slowly God showed me that I was strong enough to handle what I was going through. When my season finally changed it didn't matter where I was and even now it doesn't matter where I am because God has brought me through the valley of the shadow of death and I have to express my joy and thanks to Him in a way that is more than just words. I would yell the praise Hallelujah at the top of my lungs and people couldn't understand the intensity of my praise but I had to tell them succinctly that if you don't know my "Been Through", don't talk about my "Breakthrough!" I have to praise and worship Him in the way I do. My spirit is compelled to. **Your perspective in your story makes the difference.**

Your perspective means everything. **Proverbs 23:7 – As a man thinketh in his heart so is he.** That's why we have to watch who or what we allow into our mind. Nothing can enter your mind unless you allow it. Watch those who would tell you how to think. No one has that right and even God allows you to think and make decisions for yourself. Therefore develop your mind to the point that you are confident that it can compute efficiently, think clearly, and relate to anyone.

Whatever you constantly meditate on will materialize in your life and it will determine the fabric of your spirit. Whatever you magnify will manifest. Your thoughts attract the spiritual atmosphere of your life. Whatever you magnify will manifest. Your thoughts literally make up your spiritual body. Whatever you magnify will manifest. Your ideas expose your identity and henceforth whatever you magnify will manifest! Therefore think righteous thoughts and insulate your minds from things that's not worthy of it. Don't diminish the brilliance of who you are with things that don't bring you value. A mind is a terrible thing to waster, therefore don't waste it invest in it. It's one of your greatest commodities on this Earth.

Jesus called His disciples and **us** to be different in His greatest sermon the Sermon on the Mount. He preached what we now called the Beatitudes which called His men out. Telling them that their attitudes were supposed to be different than everybody else or they'd be in danger of not pleasing God and/or making it in to Heaven. It was that serious, refer to **Matthew 5:11-12.**

The reason behind this is perception. Jesus asked His disciples "Who do men say that I am?" The reason that He asked is because it was important to Him what people thought regarding Him. Jesus literally was doing what we call in the military a Climate Survey. A Climate Survey is a survey that is disseminated throughout an organization to get the *feel* of it. It's a mood check in a sense. Every fortune 500 company perform these self evaluations on themselves.

These types of checks should be systematic in our physical and spiritual lives. I teach in my church that we should do this with our bodies. Have you ever ran into someone that used to be thin or fit that is totally not fit anymore and acts like they don't know how it happened and when it happened? The only way a person can do this is if they totally neglect the "climate survey" of their bodies. They obviously haven't been on any real physical regiment that required them to weigh themselves weekly or monthly. I guarantee that these individuals always looked at themselves in the mirror with their clothes on, if they looked at themselves at all. With your clothes on you can miss the fact that your belly is hanging over your belt or that tires is now hanging where six packs used to be. In other words, you can miss the fact that your flesh is growing out of control. You have to inspect yourself totally naked to really understand the "climate" of your body. Every time I teach this I always hear uncomfortable laughs and that's because people are uncomfortable with the truth and would rather live a lie or a fantasy. We are uncomfortable with the subject of transparency. However we know that the truth is what really makes us free. Confidence in anything other than the truth is nothing but the spirit of deception and this spirit should not live in the body of a believer and thusly requires a change of perspective.

It's important to get an assessment of yourself in words. Jesus didn't just use his perceptual or divination skills regarding what the perception was about Him, he prompted dialogue. Refer to Matthew 16:13-17. They told Him some thought He was John the Baptist, Elijah, or Jeremiah come back to life but He asked "Who do you say that I am?" And Peter said "You are the Christ, the Son of the Living God." It pleased Jesus to hear the words because He understood where words come from and the power of words in this dimension.

Words are exposed thought. That's why we have to choose our words carefully. Proverbs 6:2 reads, *You are snared by the words of your mouth.* If you say it you're saying it because it's in you. Once you utter a succinct thought, question, or command it becomes a thing and the universe logs it and responds to it. This is why the demons or fallen angels always try to take a host body to gain access to the power of words and speech in this dimension. They don't have this power in their dimension so they have to possess a human being that is not protected by the Holy Spirit and manifest all types of evil into the atmosphere. This is part of the reason that Jesus would tell them to shut up when they tried to speak to Him before He would cast them out.

Therefore thoughts are things in the same way that oxygen and electricity are. You have to think of something before you speak it into existence. The spirit of man can be thought of is His mind, the invisible part that we consider our mentality. Your soul is contained within your spirit and could be thought of as your personality. The attributes of your personality are attitudes, emotions, and beliefs. Your soul is unique and can't be duplicated. In the same way that if someone put your soul in another host body you would still be you and act like you. If someone attached another person's arms or legs you would still act like you. Your brain or should we say spirit; sends a signal to your mouth, throat, and tongue to make an utterance. Your mind controls your physical brain which controls your physical body and when this invisible line is distorted it creates insanity such as the epileptic boy of Matthew 17:15.

The relationship between negative thoughts, stressed emotions and sin, is only now being studied. But, these relationships have long been observed. Jesus spoke often of the relationship of some illness and sin. Refer to the following scriptures for your edification; (John 9:2-3 – blindness; Matt 9:2-6; Mark 9:29, and Matt. 17:14-21. Mark 2:5 – palsy; Luke 5:20 – palsy.) Jesus explained that these type of physical illness were spiritually engineered that could only be overcome by prayer and fasting. Therefore we could surmise that some conditions and illnesses are not biological or even natural they are spiritually initiated and demonically inspired. They torment your soul which is why your personality changes and play with your mind which causes you to get confused and as a consequence become unstable.

Further references to look at to show the correlation of the matter of our heart with the words that we produce and thereby the actions that ensue are as follows:

* Sin such as Murder begins in your heart. – Matthew 5:21-26

* Adultery begins in your heart – Matthew 5:26-28; John 8

* Wickedness begins in the heart – Proverbs 6:12

* Perversity begins in the heart – Proverbs 6:14

The matter of our heart is so important to God that He says in **Proverbs 21:1-2**: *1.) The Kings heart is in the hand of the Lord, like the rivers of water; He turns it wherever He wishes. 2.) Every way of a man is right in his own eyes, But the Lord weighs the hearts.*

Our most difficult decisions are really matters of the heart and God is constantly checking our hearts to make sure it is calibrated correctly. Now you're probably asking how can we make sure that we stay delivered. We do that by following the instructions of ***Proverbs 6:3-5:***

3.) So do this my son and deliver yourself; For you have come into the hand of your friend: Go and humble yourself: Plead with your friend. 4.) Give no sleep to your eyes, nor slumber to your eyelids. 5.) Deliver yourself like a gazelle from the hand of the hunter and like a bird from the hand of the fowler.

Ensure that the strings of your heart are being pulled by the perspective of God. It doesn't matter how tough your assignment looks. It doesn't matter what kind of storm you're finding yourself in right now. Just know that God will give you grace for every assignment and provide provision for every vision.

CHAPTER 11

*W*eeds in your *G*arden

How many of you think you know a little bit about gardening? If you do let me ask you what are the main components of a garden? Or when you think of the word garden, what do you visualize? Flowers…colors? You would be right but I'm sure that most of you left out one important ingredient. And that ingredient is weeds. You're asking yourself, a garden needs weeds? Yes beloved, every garden needs weeds. Weeds are nature's healing remedy for the areas that are in a wounded, grassless, plantless state. It's God's genius way of ordaining life in the Earth. It's His way of reenergizing and revitalizing dead ground and/or misused land. I know this is news for all of the amateur gardeners out there because they just believe in digging up a bunch of dirt or chopping up a bunch of roots and just creating havoc on a piece of earth. I'm just here to say that if that is the way you have always operated, stop it. You've been digging up your blessings.

You see every square inch of a garden contains the weed seed. God designed it this way to ensure the stimulation of his Earth at all times. Some land would be barren with no growth at all if it wasn't for the weed seed. Some plant and flower seeds are scattered too far away sometimes to provide the proper stimulation to the soil in a garden or grassy area so God ensured that something would be there to stimulate it at all times. Therefore one could say that the weed seed might be the most important aspect of any garden.

Please understand that God loves gardens. As a matter of fact, I would say that a Gardener would be the best attribute to describe Him concerning us. In **Genesis 2:8** it says- *Now the LORD God had planted a garden in the east, in Eden; and there he put the man he had formed.* So our first habitation on this Earth was a garden. **Isaiah 51:3** states *The Lord will surely comfort Zion and will look with compassion on all her ruins; He will make her deserts like Eden, her wastelands like the* **Garden of the Lord**, *Joy and gladness will be found in her, thanksgiving and the sound of singing.*

God talks about us as His harvest numerous times in His word. Jesus makes numerous garden like references such as the "wheat and the tares". He referred to souls as the fertilized product of "seed" and on and on and on. My point is that most people look at weeds as a bad thing but I'm here to tell you that weeds in your garden are very necessary things and in the end benefits you.

~ Weeds Create Passion ~

A lot of us need stimulants to get into motion. Some of us don't go to church until things start going wrong. Some of us don't pray until our money start getting short. Some of us don't acknowledge God until somebody that we think shouldn't have died dies, until our child is sick, or we don't want our spouse to leave us, etc. All of these type situations are weeds. There are countless scenarios to use however I believe the point is made. Weeds are necessary and they're inherent stimulants in the garden of our life. It is something in your life that will irritate, push you and motivate you to be better. Therefore we need to do what James tells us to do in James 1. Brethren, count it all joy when you fall into diverse temptations. God is using your little setback for a comeback. Therefore be reenergized.

Beloved, simply put our God loves Gardens. Man's first home was a garden. God placed us inside of His garden and gave us complete dominion over it. The greater miracle other than the visual one we see with our eyes when we look at beautiful gardens and flowers and trees is the power that exists to enable growth. Yes that beautiful red rose is scrumptiously beautiful and smells so exquisite. Yes the field of wheat is an awe inspiring sight of God's plan of harvest and supply to mankind. The 30 foot Oak Tree is a daunting sight and the mouth watering mangoes that fall off of the mango tree is simply excellent. But what's even more awe inspiring than what is produced is the power that must be in place for the product to be produced. You see, the glory of the creator is visible in His creation. This is the reason why God instituted the Sabbath. Not to bring unnatural affection to a day but just so that man could take a day to reflect on God's awesome creation that He created in six days. God said just rest and just take inventory of the lush gardens and majestic mountains that He created. Take inventory of the natural waterfalls, seas, and oceans. Look at the array of creatures in the waters and the fowls of the air. Dream and marvel about the clouds in the sky and the sun, moon, and stars. Look at all of this and just declare the goodness of the Lord in the land of the living. It's not the day that church has to be on and what man would tell you, it's the day to remember the power behind the "garden."

Let's look at **1 Corinthians 3:5-6**

5)What, after all, is Apollos? And what is Paul? Only servants, through whom you came to believe--as the Lord has assigned to each his task. 6) I planted the seed, Apollos watered it, but God made it grow. So neither he who plants nor he who is anything, but only God, who makes things grow.

In the beginning God placed man in a Garden and in our end we go back to this garden. The beginning, the garden. The end, the garden. It bears repeating beloved. At every funeral it says ashes to ashes, dust to dust. Get it? Your flesh can't get you to heaven, but your spirit can therefore don't reap unto your flesh reap unto your spirit. God doesn't honor the flesh, He does say however, that those who worship Him must worship Him in spirit and truth.

Consider **Genesis 2:8**

Now the LORD God had planted a garden in the east, in Eden; and there he put the man he had formed.

Of course God can be described as our Creator, our Master, our King, our Father, and even our Husband. And yet I have found that one of the best ways to understand God is in the light and likeness of a simple gardener. For any reader of the Bible, the multitude of metaphors should make it clear that God is the Gardener, and we are His plantings. In fact, this analogy is so appropriate that the Bible could be renamed "Gardening by God" and it would accurately capsulate what God's will and purpose for humanity are. In short, mankind is a divine crop of spiritual beings that God plants, grows and hopefully harvests at their maturation so that more of the glorious image of God is revealed. This humble and simple relationship seemed clearly understood by the anointed and beloved John of two millennia ago.

John 15:1

"I am the true vine, and my Father is the gardener."

An interesting fact that I've learned is that even fertile soil can become too hard making it difficult for anything to grow. Clay, as a matter of fact, is rich in nutrients and has everything a plant needs. But the problem is it becomes too hard for the roots to spread and grow to receive these essentials.

> Lesson: *Leaders don't allow your style and methods and traditions to cause you to choke the life out of the seeds that are growing and have taking some kind of root.*

Lighten up leaders and ensure that you're not propagating the same legalism that the Pharisees and Sadducees were spreading two millennia ago. Remember **2 Corinthians 3:17** – *Where the Spirit of the Lord is, there is liberty!*

Consider the wisdom of the Gardener:

~ Let sleeping weeds lie ~

The proper way to tend to weeds in the natural when the time comes is to kill them at their roots but leave the soil and dormant weed seeds largely undisturbed. Meaning that in the spiritual when we start trying to fix ourselves we need to allow God to deal with our root issue. Everything that we go through has a purpose and is meant to be used therefore we shouldn't "throw out the baby with the bathwater" as they say. The water is dirty yes, but the most valuable part of the contents within the basin is the baby. There may be weeds that you need to dig up and discard but don't forget everything that you went through. Don't forget the minerals and good soil that has grown as a result of the sunshine and water that God still provided during the process. Don't forget that God was there with you the whole time. Don't try to make yourself new, let God handle that. Honestly, He's the only one qualified to do that anyway.

Every square inch of your garden contains weed seeds, but only those in the top inch or two of soil get enough light to trigger germination. The lesson behind this fact is that the closer we remain to God the more blessed we become. Even our faults and issues we should present them to the Lord. Why are you trying to hide your flesh issues, your attitude issues, your evil desires and ungodly ways? Don't you understand that God knows it all anyway? Give it to God beloved, He makes all things new. The rays of the Son will grow grace and mercy around your issues in the same way that dirt protects the weed seed. Therefore present even your issues to the Lord because it will qualify you for even more grace than you're already receiving. Think about this, the woman caught in adultery was saved because of Jesus being on the scene. If she was ashamed and decided to run somewhere other than where Jesus was she would've been stoned and never had the opportunity to change her life to be heaven bound. However because the Lord was presented with her "issues" she was offered grace.

Important reminder that what we magnify will always manifest. Therefore stop rehearsing your failures because God has already used your failures to fertilize your future. Secondly and as another reminder

don't be surprised that there are weeds there. They're necessary!

Digging and cultivating brings hidden weed seeds to the surface, so assume weed seeds are there in your life ready to erupt, like ants from an upset anthill, every time you open a patch of "ground." Ensure that your foundation is built on the firm foundation of God's Word. Dig only when you need to and immediately salve the disturbed spot with more of God's Word. In lawns, an experienced gardener will minimize soil disturbance by using a sharp knife with a narrow blade to slice through the roots of dandelions and other lawn weeds to sever their feed source rather than digging them out. We should operate spiritually the same way. The Word of God is *sharper than any two edged sword piercing even to the division of soul and spirit, and of joints and morrow, and is a discerner of the thoughts and intents of the heart* according to Hebrews 4:12.

Keep in mind that weed seeds can remain dormant for a long, long time. Therefore be cognizant of the seeds that you're sowing in your life.

Consider **Galatians 6:7 in the NIV and then Amplified**

NIV 7 Do not be deceived: God cannot be mocked. A man reaps what he sows.

AMPLIFIED 7 Do not be deceived and deluded and misled; God will not allow Himself to be sneered at (scorned, disdained, or mocked by mere pretensions or professions, or by His precepts being set aside.) [He inevitably deludes himself who attempts to delude God.] For whatever a man sows that and that only is what he will reap.

~ If you care you will Prepare ~

If you were to travel to the most beautiful locations in the world you would ensure that you dieted, saved funds got your hair done or cut, and packed your nicest outfits. Likewise, you must prepare for your Harvest. *If you care, you must prepare.* The greatest athletes prepare rigorously, that way their performance isn't left up to chance or luck which is why the Bible says in 2 Timothy 2:15 "Study to show thyself approved unto God, a workman that needeth not to be ashamed, rightly dividing the word of truth." **So start off right because you never have to recover from a good start.**

What you eat in private you will wear in public. *Therefore don't let your fruit or lack thereof expose you.* I come from a boxing background. I used to train at Shuler's Gym in West Philadelphia. Before I was able to hit the bag, my trainer, the great Jimmy Beacham, regulated me to foot work only, for three months. If I hit the bag he would shun me and not give me any pointers because it showed that I lacked patience and discipline. He wanted to ensure that my foundation was solid. He understood that how good I would become depended on my foundation; namely my form, obedience, and discipline. After three months, I was able to hit the bag under his tutelage. I realized the value of his sternness because footwork was never a problem for me after that; it was something that I literally didn't have to think about in the ring or out. I moved better than guys who boxed for many years longer than I did. Even to this day, the movement, spacing, and "sweet science" as we call it are fused into my very muscles and bones. This taught me that you can never prepare enough because preparation is never wasted.

You've got to prepare yourself for the relationship that God has for you. Some of you are asking God for deliverance, but you refuse to break the chains of bondage that you're in. You're refusing the discipline part of the process. You're refusing the humbling part of the process. I got news for you; you will never arrive in your city of promise without going through the process. God Himself is the architect of the process. Furthermore, God won't deliver you to your next phase or dimension in Him if you haven't learned the life lesson behind it. God allows different things to grow you, to teach you a life lesson that you'll need to make it through the next phase. As long as you've got pride in your heart God won't even allow you to have a hint of success. As long as you have immoral stuff going on God can't order His prosperity angel to go to work so to speak. Obedience comes before sacrifice and humility comes before honor.

Stop making bad choices and don't put your trust in a person who doesn't love themselves. There's an African saying which says; be careful when a naked person offers you a shirt. Which simply means why you would expect someone that hasn't achieved anything to be a wealth of knowledge on everything? If a person hasn't gone beyond what you've achieved in life don't place all of your stock in their wisdom. Why would you put your stock in a person that hasn't taken their own advice? A naked person can appear to be in a position of privilege for a minute but it won't be long before you realize that they are shamefully barren in content and utterly exposed. It will only take a little change of the circumstances to see that they are woefully unprepared to deal with the elements.

Surround yourself with people who are better than you, holier than you, smarter than you, richer than you and even better looking than you. If you only stay in the company of people that you're better than how will you ever grow? If you know more than every body else than there are no more levels for you to obtain and dimensions for you to arrive at in life and this should never be the case. A person who has ran their self into the ground will undoubtedly do the same to any who would attach to them. There is a saying that says it won't take long for a small man to bring a big church down to his size and the old saying that misery loves company is still true.

Don't be so quick to get your Harvest! Sometimes God will delay you because He knows that there is a storm where you're going. Remember that old saying "Act in haste, repent in leisure?" Don't make hasty decisions and choose poorly because of impatience. Patience is a virtue like the old saying says and if you are truly a virtuous woman or man then you will exercise this quality regularly. One of my favorite scriptures is Isaiah 40:31- They that wait on the Lord shall renew their strength. They shall mount up on wings as eagles, they shall run and not grow weary, and they shall walk and not faint. Wait on the Lord beloved! Never make a permanent decision because of a temporary situation. Always remember that your problems are temporary but your God is eternal.

Disappointment doesn't mean that you're not appointed. Disappointment just means that your appointment hasn't been scheduled yet. So just dig your heels in and wait a little bit longer beloved because in due season you shall reap your harvest if you faint not. Therefore keep sewing good seeds so that they can yield good crops.

Your must plant before you Harvest. Proverbs 20:4 states: *A sluggard does not plow in season; so at harvest time he looks but finds nothing.* So just because you're not seeing the results doesn't mean that God isn't working behind the scenes. God can't lie and whatever He says is yeah and amen. Don't be the sluggard of Proverbs 20:4 that is expecting something from nothing. God can't stand laziness and the fruit of laziness is lack and poverty so He doesn't even has to chastise you because the principle of the sluggard is poverty and yields its own reward. Success is earned and never given.

The world says luck favors the prepared but know this dear one; favor favors the prepared.

Larry Edward Birchett, Jr.

CHAPTER 12

*I*ndecent *P*roposal

*A man can be destroyed but he can never be **defeated** unless he wants to be. ~ Pastor Larry Birchett, Jr.*

Some of you have been paralyzed because of an experience that you've endured at one point or another in your life. Something that you've never told anybody else. I'm here to tell you that the experience you've endured was for your development not your damnation. Don't let it define you. The key to recovery and restoration in God is the ability to leave the past in the past and come to terms with who you are today. The devil will always bring up your past because he has no control over your future. The other thing you need to know is that just like a sore needs air to heal, God will readily heal what you reveal.

Twenty four years ago I endured one of these "developmental" experiences that God has used to shape me and mold me for my assignment and purpose. I want to let someone know that God had a purpose for us before anybody ever had an opinion about us, your job is to find out what that purpose is. God won't heal what you don't reveal so in this chapter release "it" and free yourself.

He knew that you were going to put yourself in a situation that was beyond your control and it would stain you but He had a plan to make your pain become your pulpit and for your latter to be greater than your former. Consider the story of Tamar and the indecent proposal that she had to deal with:

2 Samuel 13:1, 2 ~ *After this Absalom the son of David had a lovely sister, whose name was Tamar; and Amnon the son of David loved her. 2 Amnon was so distressed over his sister Tamar that he became sick; for she was a virgin. And it was improper for Amnon to do anything to her.*

How many of you know that sometimes it's what's going on in the inside of a person that's affecting them on the outside? It's not bacteria or a virus all of the time. Sometimes it's the out of alignment of their natural "man" and spiritual "man" that is literally making a person sick.

Spoiledness or always getting what you want can make your spirit sick. Especially when you're finally told no or you can't get what you want. That's why if we love our children we bring them up with some sort of structure. And sometimes we just have to say "no" in situations that are not life and death to make them understand that sometimes life will tell you no and it's okay. We have to teach them that everybody is not going to agree with them all of the time. Everyone will not think the way they think about things and some will literally come against everything that they represent and guess what? That's okay.

Sin can also make you physically sick. When you know better sin will make your head hurt, your body hurt, it'll make your internal organs hurt, it'll even make you look different. I remember that when I was about to have my first child I still hadn't told my parents and my girlfriend was already a few months pregnant and the stress of the deception was literally making me sick. To the point that I had to call both of them to come pick me up from the job that I was working at the time and I was in my 20's. I was nervous because my father was a pastor and my mother was also a very respected spiritual leader and I didn't know what to expect from them being that my girlfriend and I wasn't married and so on and so forth. By the time they picked me up my eyes was swollen like Garfield's and I got in the back of the car and spilled the beans. Immediately my eyes went back to normal and the sickness left. It was a spiritual ailment that I was dealing with.

3 But Amnon had a friend whose name was Jonadab the son of Shimeah, David's brother. Now Jonadab was a very crafty (shrewd) man. 4 And he said to him, "Why are you, the king's son, becoming thinner day after day? Will you not tell me?"

Amnon said to him, "I love Tamar, my brother Absalom's sister."

Just like Jonadab some people are not even opposed to the greatness that they see in you. They're not opposed to the call of God on your life and what God has for you. They're not opposed to even what you see personally regarding the plan that God has for your life. But what they are opposed to is where they're situated in the plan for your life.

For some people if they're not in a prominent spot in your success they'll try to sabotage your success instead of helping you reach your promise. That's why you have to listen to God for direction. But you can't do that if you don't have structure and know His voice. In your process you'll run into people that if they're not going to get credit for your next level or dimension in God they'll back off and just watch you struggle. This is even when God Himself has told them to help. All that occurs when this happens is that they'll lose their blessing and God will simply use somebody else that is obedient to His will and not their own will.

Watch your circle. The five people closest to you are a reflection of you. If one of your friends is a crack head, the other one is a drug dealer, the other one is a drunk, and the other one a womanizer, and the next is a murder, you can't sit there and tell me that you have a high moral threshold because your acquaintances show otherwise. Birds of a feather flock together. Amnon should've listened to someone other than Jonadab because he was only about the scandal.

Jonadab was 35 years old, Amnon was 22 years old, and Tamar was 15 years old. So we see a disparity of development. However age is not always an indicator of maturity and it definitely is not an indicator of spiritual maturity and integrity. Amnon had the right thought about confiding in an older man not withstanding the fact that when an older man take interest in a young girl he's sick but the other thing is that Amnon didn't realize that Jonadab wasn't really his friend. Ensure that your friend is your friend and not your "Frienemie."

Jonadab was a Frienemie. A Frienemie will know just enough about you to do you in, but they won't ever do anything contrary concerning you while they're in your presence. A Frienemie will be your best buddy when you're around but will make you look bad when you're not around because they're not really for you . Men watch who you get your advice from. If the person is carnal or "worldly" I would 9 times out of 10 take his advice as what NOT to do.

Verse 4 shows us that we should be careful. Be careful because some people PROPHECY, Some people PROPHELY, and then some people PROPHESPY so that they can PROPHELY and pretend that God gave them a word. Notice I said some people do this, not everyone.

Verse 5 says *So Jonadab said to him, "Lie down on your bed and pretend to be ill. And when your father comes to see you, say to him, 'Please let my sister Tamar come and give me food, and prepare the food in my sight, that I may see it and eat it from her hand.'"*

Ladies if he's sick, let him die and just say thank you Lord for your grace to me. Because you don't want to be with a sick person anyway. Flip the script on them and say I'd rather be with a healthy man because these men will do anything to try and trick you ladies.

Ladies a lot of men with ill intentions will try to seduce you. They'll say that I just want to help you but don't be fooled. If it's 2:30 in the morning and your phone rings and it's Johnny on the other line, let it go to voicemail. Men and women whenever the devil calls let it go to voicemail.

2 Samuel 13:6-8 *[6] Then Amnon lay down and pretended to be ill; and when the king came to see him, Amnon said to the king, "Please let Tamar my sister come and make a couple of cakes for me in my sight, that I may eat from her hand." [7] And David sent home to Tamar, saying, "Now go to your brother Amnon's house, and prepare food for him." [8] So Tamar went to her brother Amnon's house; and he was lying down. Then she took flour and kneaded it, made cakes in his sight, and baked the cakes.*

As great a man that David was the Bible clearly shows us that he lacked discernment and judgment in some areas. That's why we have to continually pray "Lord lead me not into temptation and deliver me from EVIL."

David should've been able to hear something in his son's voice to let him know that he was sending his daughter into DANGER. He should've known that Amnon was the trickster of the family and that he was indecent. But David was so beat up by his own indiscretions that he started losing confidence in his ability to discern between right and wrong. And he forgot the word of the Lord that came to him in judgment because of his own indiscretions with Bathsheba in 2 Samuel 12:11-12.

Nathan let David know that his sin wasn't secret but in spite of it, God still loved him and had taken away his sin but that he still had to pay the fine. 2 Samuel 12:13. Reader say this aloud: **If you don't want to pay the fine, don't do the crime!**

Back to Chapter 13 – We have to protect our children because some of them, just like we were, are naïve and will put themselves in situations that they themselves will not be able to control.
2 Samuel 13:8-13:

⁸ So Tamar went to her brother Amnon's house; and he was lying down. Then she took flour and kneaded it, made cakes in his sight, and baked the cakes. ⁹ And she took the pan and placed them out before him, but he refused to eat. Then Amnon said, "Have everyone go out from me." And they all went out from him.¹⁰ Then Amnon said to Tamar, "Bring the food into the bedroom, that I may eat from your hand." And Tamar took the cakes which she had made, and brought them to Amnon her brother in the bedroom. ¹¹ Now when she had brought them to him to eat, he took hold of her and said to her, "Come, lie with me, my sister."¹² But she answered him, "No, my brother, do not force me, for no such thing should be done in Israel.

Do not do this disgraceful thing! ^{13} And I, where could I take my shame? And as for you, you would be like one of the fools in Israel. Now therefore, please speak to the king; for he will not withhold me from you." ^{14} However, he would not heed her voice; and being stronger than she, he forced her and lay with her.

Verse 13 shows that she was even willing to let him have "it" as long as he went about it legally. She said look go talk to the King and you can have "this". But he started singing to her and wooing her and then finally he overpowered her and took "it" from her.

Ladies if your man don't want to put a ring on it after a reasonable amount of time and if they're truly just your friend and not friends with benefits you'll have no problem distancing yourself from them until their "sickness" is gone! Your heart should be so hidden in God's hands that they have to go to Him to get to you! Tell them to go see the King and the King will let you know that he's the right one for you.

We've got to have standards. We've got to raise our children right. Some of us have been molested, assaulted and/or raped by people close to us or just people who were **shrewder** than us as Jonadab was to Amnon as explained in verse 3 of this text and we've had to live with the guilt of the incident or act.

In 1989, due to my own lusts and perversions I found myself in a precarious situation. I was at one of my "frienemie's" house and we were watching things that we weren't supposed to watch and drinking things that we weren't supposed to drink, etc. He was older than me and little did I know that this person was struggling with a homosexual spirit. He made an indecent proposal in the form of verbally stating that he would perform oral sex on a male. I was so disgusted and of course this started a serious argument. However, due to youthful inexperience he made me think he wasn't serious and was just high or drunk or something and I believed him because he and I talked about and pursued females many times. At least I thought that we were doing this. However in my naivety and lustful ambitions I stayed at the house a little longer due to the pornographic movies that he had that I was enjoying and the females that were on their way and so on.

    I thought I could manage and handle the situation. However as I would soon find out, I couldn't. I was instead overwhelmed by the situation because in the end I wound up being sexually molested and probably abused. I will not give the details of the incident as suggested by my editing/publishing team due to the graphic nature of the incident and this is an inspirational book. But my disclaimer to everyone is to watch out for the drinks that you're served whereas they could be laced with debilitating drugs of what we call today "date rape" drugs and spirits. And yes men they do have drugs that is stronger than anything you've ever taken or done to the point that you won't even remember what happened. I couldn't even move at first. I didn't even realize that something had happened until after the event and I was able to think a little more clearly. I was beyond furious as I found myself enduring one of the most shameful experiences in my life and just like Tamar I was left desolate by the shrewdness and deceit of someone more experienced than me.

    I thought so many things all at once. I entertained thoughts that I somehow deserved this, allowed this or gave the signal to the universe that I wanted this. This incident was severely traumatic and life altering. I felt as if I were about to die, that these were the last minutes of my life. But I finally managed to move and I won't disclose the rest whereas not to incriminate myself. However you could imagine my anger and what ensued after I got my bearings. It was the grace of God that I didn't get locked up after the scenario due to my response.

I left stripped, broken, abused, destroyed, and desolate. The worst day of my life. The spirit of anger attached itself to me and I spent many years being controlled by this spirit. This scenario also messed with my self esteem and I became extremely promiscuous whereas I now understand that subconsciously I felt the more women I slept with the more of a man I was.

The only person that knew something was going on with me once I finally made it home was my mother. She just honed in that something was wrong with me. Of course I lied, because now my manhood was in question. I'd been damaged partly because of my impatience to experience things that I really wasn't ready for, my lack of integrity, lack of faith, purity, obedience and ultimately flirting and consorting with the enemy. Because even then I knew better. I'd been taken advantage of by someone shrewder than me. **1 Cor. 15:33 – Do not be misled, "Bad company corrupt good character"**

Remember this dear one, love gives lust takes. If your dating someone assess their ability to make you better. Ask yourself are they an improvement or a liability? Because love is a choice you should ask yourself can I afford to love this person? True love is never evil and will add value to your self esteem and sense of self worth. If lust is involved you'll feel like you should be hiding a part of yourself and that something has been taken from you. If you love yourself you will guard yourself from even getting in certain situations and you will guard your heart from those that will gladly abuse it. I'm sharing this in this book today because God has commanded me to share this just for you beloved. This experience vexed me and tore me so much but God gave me a peace about the whole situation that I can't even explain. I found solace in one scripture that literally brought healing to my soul. That scripture is Jeremiah 29:11 - *For I know the plans I have for you," declares the LORD, "plans to prosper you and **not to harm you**, plans to give you hope and a future.* I would cry and sob the scripture as a question to God because of the "not to harm you" portion. And He let me know that He didn't do that to me. Beloved never blame God for what man or worse you are responsible for. God is not a respecter of persons.

Don't let anybody take what you don't want to give! We live in a time where we have to watch even our own sex because of the debauchery and spiritual wickedness that is so prevalent in the world.

In my situation I learned that I wasn't the only person, namely school athlete, that he had ran the same operation on and he'd been **dealt** with before. It's one of the first times that I seriously considered murder. But God! He stopped me from ruining my life.

You've got to prepare yourself for the relationship that God has for you. Some of you are asking God for deliverance, but you refuse to break the chains of bondage that you're in. You're refusing the discipline part of the process. You're refusing the humbling part of the process. I got news for you; you will never arrive in your city of promise without going through the process. God Himself is the architect of the process. Furthermore, God won't deliver you to your next phase or dimension in Him if you haven't learned the life lesson behind it. God allows different things to grow you, to teach you a life lesson that you'll need to make it through the next phase. As long as you've got pride in your heart God won't even allow you to have a hint of success. As long as you have immoral stuff going on God can't order His prosperity angel to go to work so to speak. Obedience comes before sacrifice and humility comes before honor.

Stop making bad choices and don't put your trust in a person who doesn't love themselves. There's an African saying which says; be careful when a naked person offers you a shirt. Which simply means why you would expect someone that hasn't achieved anything to be a wealth of knowledge on everything? If a person hasn't gone beyond what you've achieved in life don't place all of your stock in their wisdom. Why would you put your stock in a person that hasn't taken their own advice? A naked person can appear to be in a position of privilege for a minute but it won't be long before you realize that they are shamefully barren in content and utterly exposed. It will only take a little change of the circumstances to see that they are woefully prepared to deal with the elements.

Surround yourself with people who are better than you, holier than you, smarter than you, richer than you and even better looking than you. If you only stay in the company of people that you're better than how will you ever grow? If you know more than every body else than there are no more levels for you to obtain and dimensions for you to arrive at in life and this should never be the case. A person who has ran their self into the ground will undoubtedly do the same to any who would attach to them. There is a saying that says it won't take long for a small man to bring a big church down to his size and another older saying that says misery loves company, which is still true.

Don't be so quick to get your Harvest! Sometimes God will delay you because He knows that there is a storm where you're going. Remember that old saying "Act in haste, repent in leisure?" Don't make hasty decisions and choose poorly because of impatience. Patience is a virtue like the old saying says and if you are truly a virtuous woman or man then you will exercise this quality regularly. One of my favorite scriptures is Isaiah 40:31- They that wait on the Lord shall renew their strength. They shall mount up on wings as eagles, they shall run and not grow weary, and they shall walk and not faint. Wait on the Lord beloved! Never make a permanent decision because of a temporary situation. Always remember that your problems are temporary but your God and if you play with fire you will get burned just like everybody else. But when you're His, you'll at least receive grace.

In the end in the decade directly after graduation I learned that he passed away in and untimely and tragic death which brought to my remembrance 1 Chronicles 16:22, *touch not my anointed and do my prophets no harm.* Judgment had been ordered regarding the offenses enacted upon me and others. I believed his sin was generational as I learned more about him. But God didn't allow me to learn of the news until after I forgave him and in the end forgave myself. Before this book only one person on earth really knew what happened.

The Holy Spirit gave me clear instructions to disclose this event because it's going to help millions of people. We have to be transparent men and women of God because if not the world will not have anyone to go to for help because we're all acting like we never went through anything. Lord have your way.

Verse 15: *Then Amnon hated her with intense hatred. In fact, he hated her more than he had loved her. Amnon said to her, "Get up and Get out!"*

It's a thin line between love and hate my brothers and sisters. What had happened is that Amnon hated himself for his weakness and couldn't bear to be around her. The other flip side is that a lot of men once they get what they want because there was no love there in the first place will discard you like a wet paper towel or paper plate. Which is why I tell all of the young women in my church that they are "fine china." They're not paper plates. You see fine china is special and you don't even take them out except for special occasions and that's how we should carry ourselves as priceless and beautiful not as worthless and of no value. People just put salt, pepper, and ketchup on paper plates and then ball them up and throw them away. Ladies and men for that fact you are worth more than that. Act like it.

The Bible says in verse 20 that Tamar lived in her brother Absalom's house a desolate woman

DESOLATE: Deserted of people and in a state of bleak and dismal emptiness.

But I'm here to let you know that God can restore everything in you that you think you've lost. God is a RESTORER. Let God get the Revenge and allow Heaven to have the last say so:

Mark 9:42 says – And whosoever shall offend one of these little ones that believe in Me, it is better for him that a millstone were hanged about his neck, and he were cast into the sea.

Leviticus 20:13 – If a man also lie with mankind, as he lieth with a

woman, both of them have committed and abomination: they shall surely be put to death; their blood (shall be) upon them.

1 Corinthians 6:9-10 – Know ye not that the unrighteous shall not inherit the kingdom of God? Be not deceived: neither fornicators, nor idolaters, nor adulterers, nor male prostitutes, nor homosexual offenders 10) nor thieves, nor the greedy, nor drunkards, nor slanderers nor swindlers will inherit the Kingdom of God.

If the scriptures stopped there we would all be in trouble but the next verse says this:

11) And that is what some of you were. But you were washed, you were sanctified, you were justified in the name of our Lord Jesus Christ and by the Spirit of our God.

How do you get washed? By admitting your weakness in the area.

Romans 8:26 – In the same way, the Spirit helps us in our weakness. (NIV)

1 John 1:9 – If we confess our sins, He is faithful and just and will forgive us our sins and purify us from all unrighteousness. (NIV)

1 Corinthians 15:33,34- Do not be misled, "Bad company corrupt good character" 34) Come back to your senses as you ought, and stop sinning: for there are some who are ignorant of God – I say this to your shame.

We're not ignorant of God so we have no excuse, so let's pray to God and ask Him for forgiveness and restoration of our mind, body, soul and spirit. They might laugh at your setback but they're going to marvel at your comeback.

Finally, on this subject there are a lot of us that will try to suppress the dirtiest moments in our lives and even act like they didn't happen. But I'm here to tell you that if you forget where you came from or what you've been through you'll never reach your destination.

A person that tries to suppress their history is like a tree that can't be watered. A person who doesn't know their history is like a tree without roots.

A man can be destroyed but he can't be defeated unless he wants to be. Never give up! Never give the enemy the gratification of feeling sorry for yourself and being defeated. Grow from your experiences, get up and start working on bringing satan's kingdom down. Jehovah Shamah, the God that is always present, has been with you through every situation you've ever been through and He had your comeback story written before you were ever born. Allow Jehovah Rapha, the God that healeth, to heal you today.

Larry Edward Birchett, Jr.

CHAPTER 13

<u>*M*atimba and *K*anya's *P*ride</u>

A bird doesn't sing because it has an answer, it sings because it has a song. ~ Maya Angelou

I looked at a PBS documentary called the White Lions once. It was about a pride of lions in South Africa. The peculiar thing about the tribe is that there were two adult sister lions named Matimba and Kanya. Matimba gave birth to two white lion cubs and Kanya had two tawny looking or regular looking cubs. As you could imagine white lions are very rare and the addition of these two cubs made it harder on the pride to blend in and hence harder to survive. Prior to these, only three white lions had survived to maturity in the wild. But Matimba, the cubs' mother, was intent on the survival of her two daughters. So the show takes you through all of the hardship and missed opportunities that the peculiarity of the cubs caused and how the two mothers handled it.

All of the show was great and I love watching and learning from God's creation and nature but there was one spiritual truth and lesson that really stood out to me regarding this story. This truth is that you're only as victorious as your last victory. There is no time to celebrate after you've resisted temptation or have won a great battle in which your spirit was afflicted. These are the times to give God thanks and mark the moment with extraordinary praise and worship which is a defense to the enemy within itself and then stay prayerful and watchful. Because as the Word of God says we should watch as well as pray.

The two white cubs matured enough to fight along with the mothers and at one point they had just fought off two nomadic male lions that wanted to kill them in order to procreate with their mothers. These nomadic lions tried to take over but Matimba, Kanya, and the white cubs fought together to fend them off. They fought off the would-be suitors and then they immediately took down a giraffe and had feasted on the giraffe and was lounging and being lazy. Immediately as they were in their deepest playful moments that had turned to slumber another set of nomad male lions came and attacked them. The result was heart wrenching because they had lasted as a unit for two decades to get to that point.

1 Peter 5:8 – Be sober, be vigilant; because your adversary the devil walks about like a roaring lion, seeking who he may devour.

> **LESSON**
>
> * Your greatest vulnerabilities come after your greatest victories.
>
> * The enemy will wait as long as he has to for an opportunity to pounce so keep your spiritual "armor" on and stay prayed up.

The whole point of this last chapter is to let you know that after you've applied all of the wisdom of God's word through this book or otherwise you should understand that the battle doesn't end there. To get where you are at right now in your life was hard if you're honest and you had to go through the "process" and this process has been designed as such to lead you into a promise that no demon in hell or man on earth can remove you from. Your process has given you a song that no man can take from you. Therefore just like the birds sing because you can. The process has given you a praise unlike any others so therefore praise God in the highest will all of your might and worship Him from the depths of your spirit.

Remember that your wilderness is just your place of preparation and once you've learned everything necessary your promise awaits you. As you go through your transition place ensure that you have solidly learned the values and necessity of humility that will lead to honor and hence allow you to utilize spiritual authority. Consider

Acts 19:
¹ While Apollos was at Corinth, Paul took the road through the interior and arrived at Ephesus. There he found some disciples ² and asked them, "Did you receive the Holy Spirit when you believed?" They answered, "No, we have not even heard that there is a Holy Spirit." ³ So Paul asked, "Then what baptism did you receive?" "John's baptism," they replied.

⁴ Paul said, "John's baptism was a baptism of repentance. He told the people to believe in the one coming after him, that is, in Jesus." ⁵ On hearing this, they were baptized in the name of the Lord Jesus. ⁶ When Paul placed his hands on them, the Holy Spirit came on them, and they spoke in tongues and prophesied.
⁷ There were about twelve men in all.
⁸ Paul entered the synagogue and spoke boldly there for three months, arguing persuasively about the kingdom of God. ⁹ But some of them became obstinate; they refused to believe and publicly maligned the Way. So Paul left them. He took the disciples with him and had discussions daily in the lecture hall of Tyrannus. ¹⁰ This went on for two years, so that all the Jews and Greeks who lived in the province of Asia heard the word of the Lord.
¹¹ God did extraordinary miracles through Paul, ¹² so that even handkerchiefs and aprons that had touched him were taken to the sick, and their illnesses were cured and the evil spirits left them.
¹³ Some Jews who went around driving out evil spirits tried to invoke the name of the Lord Jesus over those who were demon-possessed. They would say, "In the name of the Jesus whom Paul preaches, I command you to come out." ¹⁴ Seven sons of Sceva, a Jewish chief priest, were doing this. ¹⁵ One day the evil spirit answered them, "Jesus I know, and Paul I know about, but who are you?" ¹⁶ Then the man who had the evil spirit jumped on them and overpowered them all. He gave them such a beating that they ran out of the house naked and bleeding.
¹⁷ When this became known to the Jews and Greeks living in Ephesus, they were all seized with fear, and the name of the Lord Jesus was held in high honor. ¹⁸ Many of those who believed now came and openly confessed what they had done. ¹⁹ A number who had practiced sorcery brought their scrolls together and burned them publicly. When they calculated the value of the scrolls, the total came to fifty thousand drachmas. ²⁰ In this way the word of the Lord spread widely and grew in power.

The demons of hell understand power, but they only **recognize** authority. Without authority you will never be able to cast the enemy away. Your title doesn't give you power beloved. Your dress, your stature in life, your house, your car, your money doesn't equate to power with God loved ones. Those that are the most powerful amongst us are the ones that have positioned themselves in Christ, the individuals that have a relationship with Him. That's what the sons of Sceva couldn't figure out and subsequently why they didn't operate with any power. Your anointing is only as strong as your relationship with our Lord and Savior Jesus Christ. Some of the things that you're going through you're supposed to beat it easily but you haven't worked on your relationship with God. Your view of God is that of a genie that you rub and stroke when you need something. How is your relationship with Christ seriously? Do you answer His calls when He's calling you? Or do you just send His call to the missed call section? Do you go out drinking and communing with someone else when He's trying to commune with you? Are you giving His glory away to someone else making him declare that I am a jealous God!

There is a power struggle going on in the church and it's not the struggle that God has commissioned us to wage. The struggle is for prestige and self purpose instead of giving God praise and living according to His purpose. Titles don't equal power beloved. Your power is in your relationship.

Never before have I witnessed such a fiasco in our ranks with this person wanting to be called this and this person believing that they should be this or this person putting another person down because they're jealous of their title or I'm going to start my own church because I don't like the serving part of this thing, I want to be in charge! And the world is looking at us like, "Those Christians are a trip!"

You ever ask yourself why it is okay to have titles in the world but we make it a problem in the church? The answer is because we are in a God ordained institution that is to be stewarded by servant leaders not leaders that would create servants. It takes time to develop the humility necessary to understand this and there is too much immaturity in the places of spiritual government and the ripple is being felt in the natural. Generations of the immature and the unprocessed have and are rearing immature and unprocessed leaders.

I believe that we as a people need to sound the trumpet to let people know that we should not be competing we should be completing. You see the difference between power and authority is that the person who has been through all of the trials and tests and ridicule and pain have reached new levels of spiritual understanding and this almost equates to what we know as rank in the natural. These spiritual ranks have power attributed to it.

You are so much more powerful than you ever have been beloved so get yourself together and if you've been off of the battlefield I hear God saying it's time for you to suit back up and go out to battle. You're better, you're stronger, and you've been tested and tried; so your worth is far more than you could ever imagine in God and all you have to do is agree with what God is saying about you and reject what the world and your mind is telling you.

You have just been authorized to access your promise. Your blessing is right ahead of you and all that God requires of you to obtain it is to pursue it. Always remember that as long as you're operating in God you are a majority. So go forth in faith with a complete understanding that if God be for you no one can be against you. You will have battles because no blessing comes without adversity and resistance creates strength and character but God has equipped you for the warfare and you already have the victory in Him. God loves you and there's nothing you can do about it beloved so you might as well make Him proud. You've been processed for His purpose and it's in fulfilling your purpose that you will arrive at the place of your promise. So get up from where you are and fulfill your God given purpose because you have somewhere that you're supposed to be. Be encouraged as I leave you with the tips and spiritual keys necessary to access this place called promise.

TIPS AND SPIRITUAL KEYS

*   Authority is God ordained power and the God ordain portion of the definition is the most important thing.

*   Power does not produce character so God will develop your character before He develops your power. If anything too much power prematurely can reveal the lack of character.

*   You can't have true authority without character because bad conduct will undermine your authority every time and you will be a tolerated vessel that is essentially powerless.

*   The vehicle that He'll use to bring you *through* while you are in the preparation stage of understanding and utilization of His power will be that of His favor.

*   All of your crowns will be received by you down here in Earth and none will be waiting for you in Heaven if you move before God saturates and ordains your earthly activity

*.   You won't receive God's right hand of blessing until He know that your character is right. Are you going to steal His glory? Are you going to love His children like He would? Or are you going to be a fox? Can He trust you with His finances? Are you going to preach what He tells you too?

*   God has to put you through the process not only so that you can develop and know what you will do but so that we all will know what you will do.

*   Godly endowment comes with earthly battles, just like in Acts 19:15. Does the Kingdom of Satan know you? (They knew Paul, of course they knew Jesus) Why? Because they had battles with the both of them. First thing to understand about Godly endowment as an earthen vessel is that you will not have an anointing that will not be tested or used. God is not in the business of wasting a special anointing on a person who either doesn't need it or won't use it. Your anointing is given in proportion to the warfare and assignments that He's designed for you.

* Consider it an honor when God allows the enemy to come against you. It means that God believes that you are one of His champions, someone able to overcome. Don't look at it as "I'm always going through" or "here I go again." Look at it with the understanding that new levels mean new devils. For every demonic attack that I overcome there are higher levels that I am obtaining in the kingdom of God. Sometimes our tribulations are a precursor as to the amount of blessing that God has in store for us but we have to pass the test.

* You can't grab anything out of the spirit realm without actually visiting (or warring) in the spirit realm. I always say that if you want something from heaven something must first leave from this earth. What normally move the heart of God are your worship and your praise. The only worship that God accepts is that of an authentic nature because the Bible says that those that Worship Him must Worship Him in spirit and in truth. And your position is what is going to determine your condition. Your position should be on you knees and/or in submission to Him at all times.

* Matthew 16:19 And I will give unto thee the keys to the Kingdom of Heaven: and whatsoever you shall bind on earth shall be bound in heaven; and whatsoever thou shall loose on earth shall be loosed in heaven.

www.ingramcontent.com/pod-product-compliance
Lightning Source LLC
Chambersburg PA
CBHW061442040426
42450CB00007B/1172